Emelyn Washburn

The Spanish masters

An outline of the history of painting in Spain

Emelyn Washburn

The Spanish masters
An outline of the history of painting in Spain

ISBN/EAN: 9783337231866

Printed in Europe, USA, Canada, Australia, Japan

Cover: Foto ©Thomas Meinert / pixelio.de

More available books at **www.hansebooks.com**

THE

SPANISH MASTERS

AN OUTLINE OF THE HISTORY OF PAINTING
IN SPAIN

BY

EMELYN W. WASHBURN

G. P. PUTNAM'S SONS
NEW YORK: 27 & 29 WEST 23D STREET
LONDON: 25 HENRIETTA STREET, COVENT GARDEN
1884

INTRODUCTORY NOTE.

MY design in these chapters is but to give a rapid sketch of the great Spanish painters, and to express some of my love for the treasures of Spanish art; a love not begun, but deepened by the study of the galleries of Madrid. Spain is still a wonderland to the art student; a long era of religious oppression robbed it indeed of much wealth, yet it remains a land of romance and art. The enthusiastic studies of Stirling-Maxwell, Head, and Ford, have opened rich treasures to the eager student; but except their volumes (and they are all out of print), there is scarcely any thing on the subject in our English tongue. The student of Spanish art is forced to seek elsewhere his knowledge, and for a thorough study he must go back to Cean Bermudez's invaluable "Dictionary of Spanish Painters," from which I have gleaned much information, and to the amusing pages of Palomino and Ponz. Yet these works must necessarily be within the reach of but few; and this fact will perhaps excuse my venturing to sketch the great masters of Spanish painting.

E. W. W.

CONTENTS

LIST OF ILLUSTRATIONS.

I.

EARLY SPANISH MASTERS.

I AM well aware that the task I undertake in sketching the Lives of Early Spanish Painters is not an easy one. If, indeed, I were designing to give a eulogy on Velazquez or Murillo, or to draw a comparison between these painters and Titian or Raffaelle, it were easily done. But an accurate photograph, after the style, not of Maella but of nature, who never flatters, but presents men as they are—the crow's-feet and the squint, as well as the holiday smiles—is a harder task. Spain has given us no fascinating chronicler, like Vasari, to tell us how the painters dressed and ate and quarrelled and aspired in those early days. In Spanish biography we miss sadly such etchings as his, which have given vivid reality to the names of the early Italian masters. It is seldom that Cean Bermudez or Palomino does more than mention the name of an artist before the fifteenth century. There are no traces left of this early art; what escaped the ravages of the Moor has been destroyed by time, or barbarously painted over by later daubers. We meet many hard problems in this study; our knowledge is scanty, and we have to deal with theories based on foreign ideas more than original sources.   There have been great differences of critical opinion.   In the earlier day of inquiry writers on Spain were inclined to see in the early Spanish art an originality and force that now seem extravagant.   Later writers give a very disparaging outline of this age, and grant to all Spanish painters before the sixteenth century little more than a few vague ideas, inspirations from Northern or Italian art.

We must examine the history of Spanish art as we would study the life of a child who passes under the training of a careful teacher, and through slow, successive steps of mental and physical growth to its ripe manhood.

With this view of the gradual growth of art we may open the page at the point where the grey of early morning breaks on us.   Of this time a few names only survive in the brief chronicle which Cean Bermudez gives.   In the tenth century he mentions several illuminated missals, the work of Vigila, Sarracino, and Garcia.   In 1109 Beatus Presbyter illuminated a Commentary of the Apocalypse for the abbey of San Sebastian, at Gilos near Burgos. The library of the cathedral at Seville preserves the Bible of Alonzo X., *El Sabio*, a work in two volumes, written on vellum, and illuminated by Pedro de Pampeluna in the thirteenth century.   And in 1291 Rodrigo Esteban was painter to King Sancho IV., and was paid one hundred maravedis[1] for certain works of which no further record remains.

---

[1] A small copper coin no longer employed.

" Singularly enough, we have traces of a very early Spanish painter in England. The name of *Petrus de Hispaniâ* first occurs in the account of works at Westminster in the thirty-seventh year of Henry III. (1253). Mr. Gage Rokewode tells us, that when the great hall was repaired ' in 1255, he was ordered to restore the painting in the king's oratory near his bed. In 1257 the king ordered his treasurer and chamberlain to pay Master Peter de Hispaniâ, whom he retained to make pictures when he desired them, sixpence for his wages daily so long as he was employed in the king's service ; and also to pay the same Peter ten pounds for his expenses, in going with his clerk of Toulouse to parts beyond the seas and in returning, and for two shields which he had made for the king's use and brought to him at Chester.' These shields were probably enamelled, and we suspect that Peter de Hispaniâ excelled in the art of decoration." [1]

We should notice here the curious ceiling of the *Sala del Justicia*, in the Alhambra at Granada. The artist is not known, but he was probably an Italian of the fourteenth century ; perhaps, as Mr. Ford conjectures, they were executed by some renegade before the Conquest. They represent ten Moors seated in council, whence the Spaniards call this the *Sala de Tribunal*. From the varied costume and the different colours of the beards, it is probable that the figures represent the chiefs of the tribes of Granada. These pictures are painted upon leather nailed to the

---

[1] Head, p. 24.

wooden dome: a fine coating of gypsum being first laid on to receive the pigments. The colours are bright and still fresh; but in flat design, drawn first in outline in brown. The ornaments on the gold ground are in relief. The other paintings in this hall breathe the spirit of chivalry and love. In one a Christian warrior is vanquished by a Moor; in another a knight rescues some unhappy fair one from a wild man ; here they play at draughts; and in the distance we see a boar-hunt and hear the clash of the spears, as Moor and Christian sweep by on their mettled chargers. The background is a strange medley of trees, birds, rabbits, buildings—like a mediæval tapestry. In each combat the Moor is victor; and the royal shield is blazoned everywhere. "The evidence is strong that they were executed while the Alhambra was the palace of the Moorish kings. The details of the dress and arms of the Spaniards and Moors are exceedingly curious. The Christian knights ride with the lance in rest protruding through the usual notch in the shield over the right breast; the Moors use their javelins overhanded; the Christians wear rowelled spurs; the Moors have the end of the stirrup formed into a spur, and ride with short stirrups. The swords of the Moors are not scimetars, but long, straight, and broad in the blade." [1]

Cean Bermudez mentions twenty-five artists between Rodrigo Esteban and the fifteenth century. Among these was Juan Cesilles, of Barcelona, who, in 1382,

_____

[1] Head, p. 29.

painted for the Church of San Pedro at Reuss, a *retablo* illustrating the lives of the Apostles. These pictures were removed in 1557. A little earlier we find two Aragonese painters, Ramon Torrente, who died in 1323, and his pupil, Guillen Fort.

Gherardo Starnina and Dello, two Florentine painters mentioned by Vasari, were among this number. Starnina, born in 1354, was a scholar of Antonio Veneziano. When driven from Florence by a violent quarrel with a fellow-painter, he came to Castile, where, Vasari tells us, " he worked much for the King of Spain, returning thence not only rich and in great esteem, but, whereas he left Florence poor and clownish, he returned thither a rich and courteous gentleman." He was a man of much humour, with a keen sense of the ludicrous. " Vasari relates, that being ordered to paint in the Chapel of San Girolamo nel Carmine a picture of that saint learning his letters, he seized the occasion to introduce a flogging scene in which the luckless urchin who was horsed, (*fanciullo levato a cavallo adosso ad un altro*,) writhing under the lash of the pedagogue, took his revenge by biting the ear of the comrade whom he bestrode."

Dello was both painter and sculptor. He executed the terra-cotta over the door of the Hospital of S. Maria Nuova in Florence. His chief skill lay in his handling of small ornamental subjects, generally taken from Ovid. He was also a fresco painter. Vasari says that his drawing was incorrect; but that he was one of the first artists who tried to show any knowledge of the muscles of the human body. None of his work is left in Spain.

We find also in the list of Cean Bermudez the name of a Fleming, *Maestro Rogel*, probably no other than Roger of Bruges,—Roger van der Weyde, the pupil of Van Eyck. In 1445 he painted an oratory for the Carthusian Convent of Miraflores, near Burgos. It was carried away from the convent by a French general, the Vicomte d' Armagnac; in 1835 it was sold in London, and is now in the collection of the King of Holland. The subjects of the oratory are the dead Christ in the lap of his mother with Joseph of Arimathea, and St. John; on one side is the Nativity, and on the other Christ appearing to the Virgin after the Resurrection.

Maestro Jorge Ingles, possibly an Englishman, is also met with in the reign of Juan II. He painted in 1455 a *retablo* for the Church of the Hospital of Buitrago. These paintings, though in the hard, rigid manner of the time, had great merit. Among them was a portrait of the donor, the famous Marquis de Santillana, and his wife. This was engraved by Fernando Salma toward the close of the last century,

Juan Sanchez de Castro flourished in the fifteenth century at Seville. Among his works in that city were a *retablo*, since removed, in the Chapel of San José in the Cathedral; and in the Church of San Julian, a fresco of St. Christopher, which has been savagely restored. In the Convent of Santifonce, near Seville, there was formerly a painting

on panel by Sanchez de Castro, representing the " Annunciation," in which the angel was dressed in full pontifical
robes, decorated with embroideries which set all chro-
nology at defiance, while in her hand the Virgin held a
rosary and a pair of spectacles. Of his school was Juan
Nuñez, whose best work is a panel in the Cathedral of
Seville, representing the "Virgin with the dead Christ in
her arms"; on either side are St. Michael and St. Vin-
cent ; and beneath is seen the portrait of the donor kneeling in prayer. Cean Bermudez praises this picture as
equalling the paintings of Albrecht Dürer in brilliancy of
colour, minute finish, and fine cast of drapery.

Schepeler says : "So far as I observed the early Spanish school, it appeared to me to possess certain characteristics which have survived more or less evidently in the
artists of a more brilliant period. The colouring is not so
vivid as that of the old German painters, but there is in
it and about it a sort of softness which produces the effect
of a veil thrown over the picture ; an effect which we
might perhaps call breadth of colouring. This quality,
visible in most of their works, even of the subsequent
period, they call atmosphere or 'ambiente.' In the following period the warm colouring of the Venetians had
powerful charms for the Spaniards, and exercised its influence the more readily because the breadth of treatment
of the former school fell in with the peculiarities of the
latter. If we add to these qualities a broad and full
pencil, readily following the artist's glowing fancy, we

shall have seized some of the principal characteristics of
Spanish painting.

" The constituent elements of fine Spanish colour differ
from those which go to make up the analogous quality in
the masters of the Low Countries, just as the colour of the
inhabitants of the one country differs from that of the
natives of the other. The white or red skin of a Spaniard
seems to be laid over an under-surface of an olive tint,
whilst that of a Fleming covers a bright red ground.
With all the brilliancy, therefore, of Spanish colouring, it
often seems dusky to an eye not accustomed to it; and
many of the best painters appear to be deficient in positive
colour.

" There is, however, another quality which must be observed in all Spanish pictures, and that is the character of
the drapery. Even in the fifteenth century the Spanish
masters could not prevail upon themselves to compose
their drapery as stiffly as those of other nations, nor did
they do it as successfully; some one or two pieces always
show that the half oriental artist, if he was not thinking
of the light drapery of the East, could not help executing
it, and had not patience to spend much time on the execution. It is, therefore, very rare to find a Spanish picture with a cast of the drapery which is entirely pure, and
to this may be added the fact, that in most great compositions one or two figures are more or less carelessly
executed." [1]

---

[1] Beiträge zur Gesch. Spaniens, s. 109.

In 1499 Gonzalo Diaz painted for the altar of the Magdalen a small *retablo,* which was ruined by later restoration.
In 1476 we find mention of the *obra Morisca,* or Moorish
work of Garcia del Barco and Rodriguez of Bejar. This
obra Morisca was probably a stucco decoration after the
style of the Alcazar of Seville, and was used to ornament
the corridors of the Duke of Alva's castle at Barco de
Avila.

In Toledo are found the most numerous traces of the
painters of the fifteenth and the first half of the sixteenth
centuries. In 1389 Archbishop Tenorio founded the
cloisters on the site of the " Jews' Market "; these he
caused to be painted in fresco in the style of Giotto.
Among the subjects represented there, Ortiz mentions
groups of heretics burning. In 1775 the chapter caused
these remarkable and unique relics of fourteenth-century
art to be painted over by Maella and Bayeu, whose raw,
pallid colour is in poor keeping with the noble Gothic
architecture.

Juan Alfon was employed in 1418 in the same cathedral; and Juan de Borgoña painted, between 1508 and
1511, a series of pictures in the Winter Chapter-house.
" These works are well preserved, and are admirable for
their brilliant colouring and tasteful drapery. The ' Nativity of the Virgin ' is the best. St. Anna lies in a
canopied bed, and the holy babe is brought to her to
be kissed, by a young nurse beautiful as a Madonna of
Perugino."[1] In the series is the " Last Judgment," a

---

[1] Stirling-Maxwell, p. 94.

powerful and vigorous composition., These pictures bear
a remarkable likeness to the school of Perugino. The
" Conquest of Oran," painted in 1514 for the Muzarabic
chapel, is so inferior in handling to this series, that it is
hard to believe it to be by the same hand.

Pedro Berruguete was a native of Paredes de Nava, and
painter to Philip I. In 1483 he was associated with
Antonio del Rincon in painting the walls of the Sagrario
of the Cathedral of Toledo. His best work still extant is
the *retablo* of the high altar in the Cathedral at Avila.
It is three stages in height and is divided into five sides.
The first stage represents St. Peter and St. Paul in the
centre, with four Evangelists and four Doctors on either
side. The second stage has the Transfiguration in the
middle, with the Annunciation, the Nativity, the Adoration of the Magi, and the Presentation in the Temple on
either side. The last stage has in the middle the Crucifixion ; at the sides, the Agony, the Scourging, the Resurrection, and the Descent into Hell. Berruguete was
associated in this work with Santos Cruz and Juan de
Borgoña. In the Prado are nine pictures which were
executed for the Dominican Convent of Santo Tomas de
Avila ; in this work, also, Berruguete was probably assisted
by Santos Cruz.

Antonio del Rincon was born at Guadalajara in 1446.
He executed numerous works at Toledo and at Valladolid,
but no trace of them now remains. His masterpiece is
over the high altar in the village of Robledo Chavela, a

few miles west of the Escorial. It consists of seventeen
pictures on the life of the Virgin, which Cean Bermudez
praises for their " drawing, beauty, character, expression,
and excellent draperies."

Rincon painted the portraits of Ferdinand and Isabella,
"the Catholic kings"; these were formerly in the Church
of San Juan de los Reyes. In the Prado are copies of
these portraits. "With much of Holbein's hardness, they
have much of his strength, but not, however, his splendour
of colour. Both seem to have been taken when the
royal sitters were in the prime of life. Ferdinand has
the dignified presence and the fine features clothed with
'impenetrable frigidity,' ascribed to him in history. His
hair, usually described as bright chestnut, here is dark,
and being cut short, and combed over his brow, enhances
the cunning keenness of his eyes. Over a cuirass he
wears a red surcoat and black cloak, and in his hand
he holds a paper, apparently of accounts. The Queen's
portrait is no less true to history than her lord's. Her
bright auburn hair and blue eyes are among the points
of resemblance between her and our Queen Elizabeth,
recalling that Princess as she appears in an early portrait
by Holbein, at Hampton Court. But in beauty of person, as in grace of character, the Castilian queen far
excels our imperial 'vestal throned by the West.' Her
forehead is high and full, and her eyes—as yet undimmed
by weeping for her only son—softly lustrous, as they
may have been when she rode victorious into the Alham-

bra. The finely formed mouth indicates energy tempered with gentleness. Her dress is a crimson robe trimmed with gold, over which falls a dark mantle. In her hand she holds a little breviary." [1]

In the Capilla Antigua, at Granada, are two more, either copies or *replicas* of these portraits.

His son, Fernando del Rincon, and Antonio and Inigo Comontes, were pupils of Antonio del Rincon.

Francisco, son of Inigo de Comontes, was painter to the Chapter of Toledo from 1547 to 1556, the year of his death. He made himself known in his art by completing, in 1533, the high altar in the " Capilla de los Reyes Nuevas," at Toledo, after the designs of Felipe de Vigarny. His best work was the highly-finished *retablo*, with panels of the Virgin and St. Bartholomew, in the Capilla de los Torres. "Comontes was one of the best of the many artists of his age, whose whole lives and labours lay within the shadow of that great Toledan church, whose genius was spent in its service, and whose names were hardly known beyond its walls." [2]

Frutos Floris was another painter employed on the great Toledan *retablo*. His Flemish name shows his Northern birth. Juan Flamenco, Juan de Flandes, and Francisco de Ambéres were his countrymen. Juan Flamenco painted in 1496 and 1491 two *retablos* for the Carthusian convent of Miraflores. Juan de Flandes is

[1] Stirling-Maxwell, pp. 91, 92.
[2] Stirling-Maxwell, p. 149.

known through his *retablo mayor*, painted in 1509 for the Cathedral of Valencia. Francisco de Ambéres was both sculptor and painter. He was associated with Juan de Borgoña in his work on the Muzarabic chapel.

Alejo Fernandez painted several *retablos* for the Convent of San Geronimo, at Cordova, representing the life of Christ, and of the patron saint. Between 1508 and 1525 he was employed with his brother Jorge and other artists in painting and gilding the Gothic *retablo* of the Cathedral at Seville. This *retablo* was designed in 1482 by the Flemish architect, Dancart, and completed in 1526. In the sacristy are three curious paintings by Fernandez. His saints, though still disfigured by gilt diadems and halos, are better drawn than those of Sanchez de Castro and his pupils, and they possess a fine sentiment and an accuracy in imitating rich materials and other such details, that show a decided advance in art.

We come now to the name of Fernando Gallegos, born at Salamanca in the latter half of the fifteenth century. In the Cathedral at Salamanca are three fine specimens of his work: a Virgin, in dark-green robe, giving a white rose to the Child Jesus; and on either side, St. Christopher and St. Andrew. His paintings formerly in the Convent of Santo Tomas at Avila have been removed to the Archeological Museum at Madrid. In the Prado are six pictures, formerly in the Carthusian Convent at Miraflores, near Burgos. They are in the style of Gallegos, and are attributed to him. There are many paintings called the

work of Gallegos, but few of them are genuine.   Palomino
says that he was a scholar of Dürer.   His style is Flemish
and much like that of Thierry Bouts.

It is no easy task for one, who has not made a careful,
personal study of these early Spanish masters, to define
their likeness or unlikeness to the old German schools.
The Museum of the Prado possesses few if any genuine
works of these painters—they can be studied only in out-
of-the-way churches and old buildings; and there the ignorant custodians call them works of Dürer or of some
other early German artist.

II.

THE SPANISH RENAISSANCE.

WE cannot divide the history of any schools in art or literature into strictly defined stages; they merge into each other. The greatest poet of every age has been its most real man. And it is this reality that marks the periods of true art. It is a living thing. Sir T. Browne says: " Nature is the art of God "; and so art is the nature of man. Las Hilanderas of Velazquez is a product of creative power, as genuine as the marvels which Nature herself weaves out of the tints of an Andalusian day. The Cathedral of Burgos grew like the forest, the arche-type of its mysterious heights and depths of shadow. Only as we appreciate its relation to a supernatural religion can we understand early Spanish art. The Catholic idea, the feeling of the embodied existence of religion, inspires it. Raffaelle painted a Madonna or a Fornarina as the fancy seized him: Correggio passed from an Antiope to a Magdalen. "Fervent faith and religious enthusiasm made Morales a great painter:" " again, Juanes prepared himself for painting by confes-sion and communion." But even in their day the change had already taken place. They belong in devotional

15

feeling to an earlier century; although in chronological order they come much later than many half-foreign artists.

With the accession of Charles V. to the Spanish throne (1516), a change had come in literature and art. The classic tone of the Renaissance, which had made a pagan Italy, spread over the Peninsula. Foreign artists flocked to Spain, bringing with them their love of ancient art. It was a natural reaction from the ascetic tone of the early masters. This loss of cloistral religious feeling was needful; only thus could art pass from its early stage into that of the cultivated mind. It required the influence of classic art before Velazquez could achieve the "Theology of Painting," or Murillo draw the Child Jesus down to his canvas.

In this process there is, of course, a change which is at once a loss and a gain. The simplicity of early thought and feeling passes away: the artist becomes more subjective, more an ideal painter; he lives in a world of his own imagination. He loses, too, the early simplicity of utterance. His pictures recognize more stringent laws of art. When the early master drew his thorn-crowned Saviour, the "Man of Sorrows" was a divine reality to him, not an ideal god as to the artist of the Renaissance. Yet the age of true art is only the complete development of the earlier sentiment.

It is to this Transition age that we owe the beginning of the wealth of the Madrid Gallery. Those Titians, which no other collection can surpass; those myriad gems of

Italian and Flemish art, which make the Prado unequalled in any country, were the product of this era.

Not only did foreign art find its way into Spain, but for the first time we begin to hear of Spanish artists in Italy. Vasari tells us that students came from France, Spain, and Germany to the school of Perugino. "Among them," he says, "was Giovanni Spagnuolo, called *lo Spagna*. He was a better colorist than any of the scholars Pietro left at his death. He would have settled at Perugia after Pietro's death, had the envy of the painters of that city, never friendly to foreign artists, not persecuted him so sorely that he was driven thence to Spoleto. There his virtue and ability won for him a wife of good family; he was also made a citizen of Spoleto; Giovanni executed sundry works there and in other cities of Umbria. At Assisi he painted the altar-piece for the chapel of Santa Catalina, in the lower church of San Francesco; the work was executed for the Spanish Cardinal Egidio. Another of his pictures was a San Damiano; he painted, also, for the church of Santa Maria degli Angeli, certain half-length figures the size of life; these are in the small chapel where St. Francis died; they represent some of the companions of St. Francis, with other saints, all full of life; in the midst of all is St. Francis himself, a work in rilievo."

Next to Raffaelle, Giovanni was the most distinguished of Perugino's scholars. There are none of his pictures in Spain.

Pablo de Aregio and Francisco Neapoli painted, in 1506, the doors of the *retablo mayor* in the Cathedral of Valencia, representing six subjects taken from the life of the Virgin.   Philip IV. said, on seeing them many years later, that "the altar was silver, but its doors were gold."   The "Adoration of Shepherds and of Kings" are the finest and most striking of the series.   These painters' style recalls that of Lionardo da Vinci, and they have therefore been considered as pupils of his,   They are painted in a Florentine manner.   The walls were also painted in fresco by these artists, but they were improved in 1674.

Pedro Francione, about the year 1521, is also mentioned as a painter of great merit.   His works are still to be met with in certain Neapolitan churches.

Alonso Berruguete was born at Paredes de Nava, near Valladolid, about 1480.   "He began life as an '*Escribano del crimen*' to the Chancelleria.   From the desk of chicanery he passed into the noble studio of Michael Angelo."   In 1503, we find him mentioned at Florence among the students of the Cartoon of Pisa.   Vasari speaks of a picture of Fra Filippo Lippi, 'which, after his death, was very well carried forward (*tirata assai ben inanzi*) by Alonso Berruguete'; but it was completed by other artists after the latter's departure from Spain.   Like Michael Angelo, Berruguete was architect, sculptor, and painter.   His style of architecture was that of the Spanish Renaissance, the *plateresque*, so called from the florid ornament which overlaid the work.   Much of the wide-spread growth of Italian art was due to his influence. He was one of the chamberlains of Charles V., and died in 1561. His chief work was in sculpture. In 1526 he erected the high altar for the Church of the Benedictines, in Valladolid. The height of this altar was fourteen yards and a half; its breadth, ten yards. The figures were carved in walnut wood and yew, the rest in pine. It was highly gilded and coloured. It was divided into two stories, each supported by twenty columns, the lower Corinthian: bas-reliefs or saintly figures in niches filled the space between the columns; the cornices and all parts where ornament might rest were carved with luxuriant flowers, foliage, and animals. St. Benedict, in the act of blessing, carved and painted the size of life, was the central figure. On either side were pictures representing the "Nativity" and the "Flight into Egypt." In the upper stage, the Virgin was soaring up to heaven, accompanied by angels. Above the whole rose a crucifix. "At Toledo, he was chosen in 1539, with Felipe de Vigarny, to carve the upper stalls of the choir, of which he executed one half, and likewise the archiepiscopal throne, over which hovers an airy and graceful figure, carved in dark walnut, representing our Lord on the Mount of Transfiguration, and remarkable for its fine and floating drapery."[1] Berruguete was employed by Charles V. at Madrid, and on his new palace in the Alhambra at Granada. One of the last and finest of Berruguete's works is the monument of the Cardinal

---

[1] Stirling-Maxwell, p. 144.

Archbishop Juan de Tavera, in the Hospital of San Juan Bautista at Toledo.

" On a richly decorated sarcophagus the great church-man lies in his mitre and robes ; his gloved hands are crossed on his breast, and his fine and venerable features —worthy of a master's chisel—wear the pure, placid expression which belongs to ' the dead that die in the Lord.' " [1]

It is in handling such a subject as this that the sculptor of the Renaissance is master. He finds here no temptation to display his newly acquired anatomy. His only aim is to seize the emotion in its moment of transition to triumph or resignation, or to the calmness of death. Sculpture, above all arts, seems in its idea as well as its materials to be fitted for the expression of repose. It embodies the beauty of calm thought, of strength undisturbed by passion, of purity and joy ; and any intrusion of another element, of the painful, the violent, destroys its charm. While in painting we delight in the most intense emotion, we seek in stone the realization of that loftier state after which we are always aiming in vain. It is the lack of this which makes so much of the work of the sculptors of the Renaissance a disappointment to us. It is beauty, but beauty in conscious degradation, and the whole expression leaves on us an impression of painful incongruity. Their genius seems more akin to painting than to sculpture. It was here, above all, that

---

[1] Stirling-Maxwell, p. 144.

Berruguete's genius showed itself, if we may believe the contemporary accounts; for but little trace of his paintings is left in Spain. "For the stiff, angular style of the earlier masters, and their lean haggard figures—whose age could be guessed at only from their sizes—he substituted the free outlines and rounded contours of Italy. Pompeyo Guarico's rule for drawing the human form, which gave nine times the length of the face to the whole figure, had been followed till Vigarny changed the proportion to nine times and one third. Albert Dürer made it ten. The practice of Berruguete, founded on his studies of the antique, fixed it at ten and one third. His statues, which are generally highly finished, display much of the manner of this great master, in their grand and noble forms, and well developed though somewhat overcharged anatomy. In painting his best works were executed for the Cathedral of Palencia and the Church of Ventosa." [1]

It is during the latter part of the reign of Charles V., from 1548 to 1553, that Palomino places Titian's visit to Spain. Cean Bermudez, on the other hand, says that Titian was there in 1535, when the emperor was on the eve of setting sail for Tunis. The best evidence, the letters written by Pietro Aretino to Titian, and his other friends, from 1530 to 1555, although they compose a monthly chronicle of the painter's movements, make no mention of a journey to Spain. We may, therefore, conclude that he never travelled out of Italy, except on the

---

[1] Stirling-Maxwell, p. 145.

occasions of his visits to the Imperial Court at Augsburg and Vienna in 1548 and 1550. It is impossible to say which of Titian's pictures, out of the enormous number now at Madrid and the Escorial, were executed in Spain ; many were purchased by Philip III., and some, as we know, came from the collection of Charles I.

To this period we owe the *Comentarios sobre la pintura* of Don Felipe de Guevara, published by Ponz in 1788. They were "written in his old age to amuse the tedious hours of sickness, and consist chiefly of anecdotes of the painters of antiquity gleaned from his classical learning, and interspersed with recollections of travel. They were dedicated to Philip II., whom Guevara exhorts to make his galleries accessible to lovers of art, ' for,' says the old scholarly soldier, ' painting and sculpture, in my opinion, are in some sort like riches, which Boëthius hath said are fruitless and of no effect when heaped together and hidden, but not so when they are shared and imparted."' Don Felipe was the grandson of Don Ladron de Guevara, Lord of Escalante and Treveño. He was an amateur painter of much ability, and a diligent scholar. He made the acquaintance of Titian in 1530, while with the emperor at Bologna. He died in 1553.

Gaspar Becerra was born at Baeja in 1520. Like Berruguete, he was both painter, sculptor, and architect. He studied under Michael Angelo, and was employed with Vasari in some work at the Vatican. Whilst there, he is

---

' Stirling-Maxwell, pp. 153, 154.

said by Vasari to have painted a " Nativity " for the Trinità del Monte. Few of his paintings have been preserved; he is best known through his sculpture. There is still in the Cathedral of Burgos his exquisite little figure of St. Sebastian. In the Church of San Isidro, at Madrid, is a figure carved by his hand. But "his most heroical work of sculpture and the crown of his studies," says Palomino, "was the image of Our Lady carved for Queen Isabella, de la Paz," and now in the Church of San Juan del Mercado at Valencia. Wishing to present an image to the order of St. Francis de Paula, she chose Becerra as sculptor. Twice he attempted to realize his ideal conception of the divine beauty; but each time he failed. Weary with his labour, worn by watching, as he sat one night by the fireside, he fell asleep; he was aroused by a voice saying : " Awake and rise, and out of the log, blazing on the hearth, shape the thought within thee, and thou shalt obtain the divine image." He arose instantly, seized the brand, and quenching the flame, carved out his thought, which grew beneath his chisel into a "miracle of art, and became," says Palomino, "the portentous image of Our Lady of Solitude, to this day had in reverence, in which are expressed beauty, grief, love, tenderness, constancy, and resignation, and which, above all, is the refuge of our sorrows, the succour in our ills, the solace of our toil, the dispenser of heavenly mercies."

But the greatest work of Becerra is the high altar of the cathedral at Astorga, "perhaps his masterpiece; it is one

of the most remarkable of its kind in the Peninsula, but
unfortunately it has been much repainted. It is divided
into three parts; the framework of the under story is supported by Berruguete pillars; the second tier has fluted
columns and enriched bases; the third, pilasters in black
and gold. The carvings represent subjects in the life of
the Saviour and Virgin; observe especially the Pietà, the
Ascension, and Coronation of the *Santissima*, and the five
recumbent females and *Michael-Angelesque* 'Charity.'
These nudities gave offence, and were about to be covered, when the *consejo* of Madrid interposed. These
grand carvings are very Florentine and muscular." [1] The
crucifix in the *retablo* of Medina del Campo is also the
work of this master.

Becerra died in 1570.

The best known of his pupils are Bartolomé del Rio-
Bernuis, Francisco Lopez, Geronimo Vasquez, and Miguel
Barroso, who has left some admirable work at the Escorial.

Pedro Machuca, a contemporary of Berruguete, also
studied in Italy. He was for some time at Granada, in
charge of the works in the Alhambra. Like Berruguete,
he united in himself the three branches of art—architecture, painting, and sculpture. Some of this latter work
still remains in Granada. Near the gate of the Alhambra
is a noble fountain, decorated with fine bas-reliefs. Over
the door of the Hospital del Sangre, at Seville, are alto-
rilievos representing Faith, Hope, and Charity.

---

[1] Head, pp. 53, 54.

In a manuscript of Cean Bermudez published at Madrid in 1802, there is an account of an early school of art which arose in Zaragoza during the fifteenth and sixteenth centuries; the earliest known Aragonese painters, Ramon Torrente and Guillen Fort, were of the fourteenth century; and we hear of no more art in Aragon until we come to the name of Bonant de Ortiga in 1457. He was employed by Don Ramiro de Fuñes, Lord of Quintos, to paint a *retablo* of St. Simon and St. Jude for the Church of San Francisco, at Zaragoza. Ortiga was painter to the deputies of Aragon.

But the real founder of the Aragonese school was Pedro de Aponte, a native of Zaragoza. He brought back with him from Italy the style of his masters, Luca Signorelli and Ghirlandaio. He was employed by Juan II. of Aragon to paint the *retablo* of San Lorenzo. He followed Ferdinand V. to Castile in 1479, and was by him appointed *pintor da camara* to the "Catholic Kings," by whom he was held in great esteem, and whose portraits he afterward painted.

Another fresco painter whose influence on early Aragonese art was very great, was Tomas Pelegret, a native of Toledo. He was a pupil of Polidoro da Caravaggio at Rome about 1520. On his return to Spain, during the reign of Charles V., he settled at Zaragoza, where he worked much in chiaro-scuro. He had many pupils, chief of whom was Cuevas, a native of Huesca. This Cuevas executed several works in black and white for the sacristy of the Cathedral of Huesca.

Mention should be made of several foreign painters whose influence ,on this period of Spanish art was very marked.   Among these was Michael van Coxcyen (usually called Coxis), born at Mechlin in 1497.   He studied for some time in Italy, and was called the " Flemish Raffaelle," although he retained a very strong Flemish spirit and style.   There are few of his works in Spain.   The most important are an " Assumption of the Virgin " (No. 3,000) and a St. Cecilia (No. 1,299), in the Museo del Prado. Some of the heads are fine, and the little fair-haired angel is very pleasing.   " A copy of the great picture, the 'Adoration of the Lamb,' by the Van Eycks, which was executed for Philip II. of Spain, is full of merit as regards the life-size figures, but is greatly inferior in those of a smaller scale." [1]

Frans Frutet, another Fleming, is known only through certain pictures painted at Seville about 1548.   His countryman, Pedro Campaña, or *El Maese* Pedro, was born at Brussels in 1503.   He studied for some time in Italy.   His greatest Spanish painting, the " Descent from the Cross," in the sacristy of the cathedral at Seville, bears the date of 1548.   In spite of a certain harshness and gloomy colour, it is a grand picture.   Murillo used to stand for hours before it, " waiting," he would say, " until those holy men should take down the Blessed Lord," and by his own wish he was buried beneath it.   Pacheco feared to be alone in the dark chapel where it hung (*temiendo estar solo in una*

---

[1] Kugler : Handbook, Flemish and Dutch Schools, p. 235.

capilla oscura). "In his 'Purification of the Virgin,' in the chapel of the Mariscal of the cathedral, we find the harsh stiffness of the 'Descent' softened to ease and beauty and an Italian suavity of tone. Raffaelle himself rarely designed a figure more graceful than that of the fair-haired damsel descending some steps to the left, who contrasts well with the beggar sprawling beneath—a study from the streets—that, doubtless, did not escape the eye of Murillo. The other smaller devotional pieces in the same altar, and the forcibly painted half-length portraits of the Mariscal Don Pedro Caballero and his family are also works of Campaña."[1] Seville contains several other of his works. He died at Brussels in 1580. His son, Juan Bautista Campaña, was also a painter at Seville.

Sir Antonis Moro, known in Spain as Antonio Moro, was born in Utrecht in 1525. He came to Spain in 1552, where Philip II. distinguished him most highly. The king's favour, shown him openly, caused such jealousy among the courtiers that he narrowly escaped being cast into the prison of the Inquisition on the charge of heresy. He took refuge in Brussels, where he spent some time. He died at Antwerp in 1588. It is on his merit as a portrait-painter that Moro's fame rests. Kugler says: "His truthful feeling, good drawing, masterly and careful painting, and transparent and admirable colour rendered him one of the best masters of his time. The portraits of his middle period are distinguished by their warmer and more

---

[1] Stirling-Maxwell, p. 123.

vigorous colouring from the paler and less carefully finished works of his later time." In the Museo del Prado are thirteen portraits by Moro. Among these is a fine likeness of Catharine of Portugal, No. 1485; a striking picture of Pejeron, a jester of the Count of Benevente (No. 1483); and " a superb portrait of our Bloody Queen Mary. The painter was sent to England expressly to paint this picture by Charles V., previous to Mary's marriage with Philip II." (1554).

The paintings of Antonio Pupiler, another Fleming employed by Philip II., were probably burned at the Pardo. Cristobal of Utrecht was also employed in Spain about this time. Ferdinand Sturm, or Sturmio, was a foreigner, perhaps a German. " He painted for the Chapel of the Evangelists in the cathedral nine pictures on panel, one of which is signed, ' *Hernandus Sturmius, Ziriczecensis faciebat*, 1551.' The centre compartment represents ' St. Gregory Saying Mass,' the panel above it the ' Resurrection of our Lord,' and those at the sides and below ' the Four Evangelists and Several Saints.' The figures are designed with some grace and freedom : the colouring is good, and affords, perhaps, the earliest example of the fine brown tones peculiar to the school of Seville." [1] Among the saints are the figures of Santa Justa and Santa Rufina, the patron-saints of Seville, whom we meet on the canvas of almost every painter. They were potters, living in the gypsy suburb of Triana

---

[1] Stirling-Maxwell, p. 127.

in 287. In a holy rage they broke to pieces the statue of the Venus of the Sevillians, as it was carried in solemn state. For this outrage they were scourged with thistles, and forced to walk barefoot in the Sierra Morena, then brought back to Seville. Justa was starved to death in a dungeon, while Rufina was cast into the arena to be devoured by a lion. On the lion's refusing to harm her she was beaten to death by the savage votaries of Venus. Sturmio represents the virgin-martyrs in the usual conventional manner, as two fair maidens who carry each a palm branch, and bear between them the Giralda, or Moorish belfry of Seville. At their feet lie some earthen pots, symbolic of their humble trade. The tower is an exact copy of the Giralda, in its old form, before it was *improved* by later architects. " Their hands are painted with great care, and their rings, brooches, and ear-rings are remarkable, not only for their exquisite finish, but for their beauty as pieces of jewelry, in which the gems are not less lustrous than Da Vinci's rich ruby on the forehead of Lucrezia Crivelli—' La belle Ferroniere ' of the Louvre." [1] " In all these figures," says Cean Bermudez, " there is an expression and lofty character ; the drawing is correct, and the attitudes are highly devotional ; the colouring is good, and the execution elaborate, like that of many Italian pictures of the time." These paintings were executed for Don Gomez Carillo di Albornoz, who, in his will, mentions the artist, calling him a remarkable painter (*pintor singular*).

---

[1] Stirling-Maxwell, p, 128.

III.

THE MIDDLE PERIOD OF THE RENAISSANCE.

AMONG the artists of this age which Head calls the "middle period of Spanish painting," Luis de Morales stands wellnigh alone, a survival of the olden time, and inspired by that religious sentiment which the mediæval church developed so powerfully. The artists of his day, followers of the Italian Renaissance, had lost that earlier feeling of an "objective presence" which Morales breathes forth in the very spirit of Fra Angelico and of the early Italian painters. Christianity gave to those masters certain ideas, which permeated their thought, feeling, and life. The mystery of God in Christ brought him nigh to the heart of humanity, yet spiritually and purely; and nature was the mystic shrine that pointed to the Invisible. Painting with them transcended the material vehicle ; it was charged with spiritual meaning. So in the Gothic cathedral the arch and the tapering spire were the symbolic fingers, that pointed to an embodied, incommunicable beauty. And with all their sombre colouring and defective drawing the pictures of the "divine" Morales leave on you the impress of reality— truth to their ideal.

The age of Athens was that of living art. The Greek mind, the most beautiful intelligence that the world has seen, embodied in perfect form the ideas of its religion; and embodied them with equal perfection in the sculptured finish of Sophocles, the marble of Phidias, or, we may presume, in the lost paintings of Apelles. But with the Spanish Renaissance there was no longer any living faith. Their artists sought for grand effects, and, as in much of our contemporary American and English art, the result was affectation. Minuteness of finish in parts, sensuous form above idea—in a word, artifice not art, these were supreme; and it was not until the next century, that the true Spanish genius burst its foreign fetters and blazed forth in Velazquez and Murillo.

Luis de Morales was born at Badajoz about 1509. He probably studied his art at Toledo, but he seems to have passed most of his life in Estramadura: few of his works are found elsewhere. About 1564, he was summoned to court preparatory to employment at the Escorial. He presented himself in a magnificent dress, so little fitted to his condition, that the king, displeased with his apparent arrogance, at first dismissed him with a sum of money. Philip's anger was appeased by the painter's assurance that he had spent all he had that he might not disgrace the king's presence. He executed, however, no work at the Escorial; the only remains of this time is a " Christ Bearing the Cross," presented by the king to the *Geronimos* at Madrid. After his return to Estramadura his eyesight failed him, and he grew very poor. Cean Bermudez discovered in the archives of the Cathedral of Frexenal, a note to the effect that in February, 1575, Morales sold for the sum of one hundred ducats certain vines in the Vega of Merida. In 1581 the king, on his return from Portugal, stopped at Badajoz, where he saw the painter in very different state from that in which he had appeared at court. " You are very old, Morales," he said. " Yes, sire, and very poor," answered the artist. Philip then ordered a pension of two hundred ducats to be paid him out of the crown rents of the city—" for dinner." " And for supper, sire ? " asked Morales. This happy reply gained the painter another hundred ducats. " Here may be seen," says Palomino, " the liberality of that great monarch, and the discreet wit of the vassal in profiting by the occasion, and speaking at the right time, which is a great felicity." Morales died five years later, in 1586. Badajoz has named the street in which he lived after the great painter.

His favourite subjects were Saviours crowned with thorns, and the *Madonna dolorosa ;* he finished highly, and was called the Parmigianino of Spain. His fault of drawing was an excessive length of proportion, and his colouring was often too dark. He sometimes painted his Ecce Homos without the crown of thorns, or the reed in the Saviour's hand: Pacheco blames this negligence most severely.

Morales bears the title of El Divino, not from his choice

of subjects, for no artist then painted other than sacred subjects, but because of his perfect execution, which was considered divine. His pictures show the impress of the German and Flemish schools; the stiff drapery, the careful finish of detail, each hair elaborated, each line perfect; a worthy follower of Fernando Gallegos, and probably a pupil of that master.

We must distinguish two periods in his style. In the first we find a large and noble treatment, and a wider range of subject, while in the second the painter restricts himself to three subjects: the Ecce Homo, the Pietà, and the Christ at the Column : compositions in which he introduces one or two figures only. In this second period we find an almost exaggerated minuteness of finish, a brilliant colour, but with an over-delicacy of feature, and melancholy grace ; it is the charm of the miniature. We find, too, a knowledge of anatomy and fine gradation of tones, with modelling that is correct, if often hard.

In the Prado are six pictures attributed to Morales. As we gaze on the thorn-crowned Ecce Homo (No. 847), we behold the King, who was born in a manger, who came in the form of a servant, who wore his crown of thorns on Calvary. No. 848, *La Virgen de los dolores*, is a characteristic example of Morales—"the drooping Mater Dolorosa, wan and weary with unutterable anguish." No. 849 represents the " Circumcision." It bears a strong likeness to the paintings of the early Florentine school ; the maidens bearing lighted tapers to the temple are very

beautiful. No. 850, a Virgin and Child, recalls again the
Florentine manner. No. 403, Christ Crucified between
Two Thieves, is in Morales' first manner. In the Academy
of San Fernando is a fine Pietà, and in San Isidro el
Real, a " Christ and St. Peter," and a " Christ at the Col-
umn," a grand picture, scarcely seen in the dim light.

In the *Musco Provincial* at Toledo are two exquisitely
finished works of Morales—a " Christ," and a " *Virgin de
la Soledad.*" In the sacristy of the Church of Asuña is a
Christ by Morales; and in the Convent of the Military
Order of Benedictines, at Alcantara, over the high altar,
are some injured works of this master. Of these the best
are a " St. John," a " Pentecost," " An Apostle Reading,"
and a noble " St. Michael." At Badajoz were formerly
the best examples of Morales in Spain. But the French
stripped the convent of its chief treasures, and those remaining have been restored. The " Crucifixion " is the
most important.

In the village church of Arroyo del Puerco, a wretched
village between Merida and Placenza, are " sixteen of his
grandest works, which, though noticed in the Dictionary
of Cean Bermudez—Soult's hand-book for Spain,—escaped the keen glance and iron grip of that picture-pilfer-
ing commander, whose troops long occupied the place.
The best of them are the grand 'Christ and Joseph of
Arimathea,' 'St. John,' and 'Christ Bound,'—three-quar-
ter length,—'Christ at the Column,' and the 'Descent
from the Cross.' Though chilled and dirty, they are, at

least, pure and uninjured either by care or neglect." [1]

In the Louvre were three pictures of Morales, of which a writer in the *Kunstblatt* of 1838, says : "Fervent faith and religious enthusiasm made Morales a great painter; his countenances of Christ breathe nothing but the most sublime expression of self-sacrifice and resigned love. The features are thin, but they are delicate and noble, and always bear the stamp of that divine humility with which our Redeemer bore the insults of the soldiers and the shame of the cross. This character of resignation is visible after death, and a wonderful expression is concentrated in the cold head on which the Virgin gazes in her lap, whilst she checks the cry of grief because she holds in her arms the Saviour of the world.[2] The colouring of Morales is warm and brilliant. His Christs remind us of a Descent from the Cross by Quintin Metsys, in the Museum of Antwerp ; but his conception is far more sublime, and his execution much more earnest in feeling than that of the Flemish master. Morales might be called the Spanish Perugino, since with him it was that pure Christian feeling ceased in the school of Castile."[3]

" With regard to the works of Morales in private collections elsewhere, especial notice should be taken of the painting in the possession of the Duke of Dalmatia; but I do not know whence it came. The subject is one constantly selected by the artist—the body of Christ taken

---

[1] Stirling-Maxwell, p. 229.
[2] This Pietà is now in the Palace of San Telmo at Seville.
[3] Head, p. 57.

down from the cross; or, what is called in Italy, a ' Pietà.'
The figures are half-lengths, the work is exquisitely finished, and evidently with a most careful study of nature.
The features are too thin, and the chins pointed; the
marks of physical suffering are not softened in the least
degree, but are rather exaggerated. Thus, the thorns
piercing Christ's head are painfully minute and true; one
comes out again from beneath the skin, and two others
show externally the blue mark occasioned by their having
been pressed by main force into the flesh." [1]

Morales left a son, Cristobal Morales, a pupil and a poor
imitator of his father. His only scholar of merit was
Juan Labrador, an admirable painter of fruits and
flowers.

Luis de Vargas, like Morales, was a devout son of the
Church. His religion inspired his art. We are told that
he was constant in confession and communion; wore the
haircloth shirt, and subjected himself to the severest dis-
cipline. Cean Bermudez places his birth in 1502, and his
death in 1568. At his death there were found in his
chamber the scourge with which he had disciplined himself; and a coffin, in which he was wont to lay himself and
meditate on death and the future life. But in spite of his
ascetic spirit, he was a keen humorist; and there are several anecdotes told of him. He was once asked, by a
friend, his opinion of a poor picture of " Christ on the
Cross." " Methinks," answered Vargas, " he is saying:

[1] Head, p. 59.

' Forgive them, Lord, for they know not what they do.' "

He studied first at Seville under Diego de la Barrera, a pupil of Alejo Fernandez. While there he painted much on the coarse *sarga*, a loosely woven cloth somewhat like bunting, These *sargas* were used as curtains for the altars in Holy Week ; or as hangings for walls of palaces, and as naval ensigns. The colours, simply wet with water, were applied to the cloth, which was then washed over with a liquid gum. This style of painting required a correct eye and free, bold handling. It was an admirable training for the beginner in art.

De Vargas, however, soon found his way to Italy, where, from his later manner, he is supposed to have studied under Pierino de Vaga. On his return to Spain he settled at Seville. His earliest work there was the *retablo* in the Chapel of the Nativity. "The Virgin Mother might have been sketched by the pure pencil of Rafael; the peasant who kneels at her feet, with his offering of a basket of doves, is a study from nature, painted with much of the force and freedom of the later masters of Seville ; and many of the accessories, such as the head of the goat dragged in by a shepherd, and the sheaf of corn and pack-saddle which lie in the foreground, are finished with Flemish accuracy."[1] "But his most celebrated picture is that commonly called ' La Gamba,' from the prominence in the composition of the leg of Adam. It represents, as we are told, the tem-

---

[1] Stirling-Maxwell, pp. 309, 310.

poral generation of Christ, and it certainly is a work of
great merit, though it is not easy to see it properly where
it hangs; one figure of a child on the ground is peculiarly
beautiful, and almost rivals the matchless Cupids of
Raphael." [1]   Luis de Vargas painted also a series of
Sevillian saints and martyrs in the niches of the Giralda,
or tower of the cathedral.   There are few traces left of
this work: only on the north side, the faded pictures of
Sts. Justa and Rufina, Sts. Isidore and Leander, and the
" Annunciation of the Virgin."   On the outer wall of the
court of orange trees is a fresco of " Christ Bearing the
Cross" or the *Calle de Amargura*—(Way of Bitterness);
this picture is sadly injured; it is commonly called *El
Cristo de los Azotados*, from the custom of criminals stop-
ping to pray before it on their way to punishment.   In
the Church of Santa Maria la Blanca is a fine *retablo*,
having as a central panel a " Pietà "; on one side " St.
Francis receiving the Stigmata," and on the other the
portraits of Francisco Ortiz and his wife, the donors of
the painting.   It is in Seville that Luis de Vargas must
be studied.   The Prado has not one of his paintings, and
outside of Spain he is little known.   It was de Vargas
who, more than any other painter, brought into Seville
the knowledge and love of Italian art, and an acquaintance with the better processes of oil and fresco painting.
The best known of his pupils were Antonio de Arfian
and Luis Fernandez, the master of Pacheco, Herrera El
Viejo, and the Castillos.

---

[1] Head, pp. 67, 68.

It is to this period that the great Valencian painter—Vicente Joanes—or, as he is commonly called, Juan de Juanes, belongs. It is supposed that he was born at Fuente de Higuera, in 1523. He probably studied in Italy, and on his return to Spain, established a school of painting in Valencia. Juanes is a true representative of his class,—the mediæval Spanish painter. His religion inspired his art. Out of the holy heart, the faith strengthened by communion, there rises that face of a suffering Redeemer, a Christ who shall sit on no golden throne, but rule only in meekness and love.

Juanes' noblest pictures of the Christ are in Valencia. " Perhaps the best is that in the Church of the Franciscans, whose insignia,—the five wounds,—still appear on the rich frame. The background of the picture is gilt; the brown hair and beard of our Lord are painted with all the minuteness of Morales ; he wears a robe of violet colour, peculiar to Juanes, and a red mantle; and in his right hand he holds up a sacramental wafer, and in his left is the cup. This cup of agate, mounted with gold and enriched with gems, is believed to be the identical vessel used by the Saviour himself at his Last Supper; it once belonged to the convent of San Juan de la Peña, and is still the pride of the cathedral treasury, and is well known in Spain as the ' Holy Chalice ' of Juanes." [1]

Many are the traditions of his devout feeling and fervid faith. He partook, fasting, of the communion before be-

---

[1] Stirling-Maxwell, pp. 360, 361.

ginning the picture of a sacred subject. Among other
legends is one connected with a picture of the Virgin,
painted for the Jesuit convent. (This disappeared during
the War of Independence.) On the eve of an Assump_
tion-day, so the legend runs, the Holy Virgin appeared in
a dream to Fray Martin Alberto, a Brother of the convent,
and desired that her picture be painted, in all the glorious
beauty then revealed to him, arrayed in white robe and
blue mantle, at her feet the crescent moon, while from the
clouds above the Eternal Father looked down, and the
mystic dove hovered over her, as the Divine Son
placed the crown on her head. Fray Martin chose
for the task Juanes, whose confessor he was. The
painter went to his easel, as a priest to the altar, purified
and strengthened by fasting and prayer. But in vain he
sought to draw the glorious vision down to his canvas.
Day after day he laboured ; holy men prayed with him,
until, at last, his faith bore its fit fruit in the miraculous
picture of the Virgin, "La Purisima," which long hung
over the altar of the "Immaculate Conception." Like
Morales, Juanes was a type of the mediæval painter ;
grave and austere in his manner, sometimes stiff in drawing ; yet with a brilliancy of colour and power of expression
rarely equalled among those early painters. In the Prado
are eighteen pictures attributed to him. Nos. 749–753, a
series of the life of St. Stephen, are very fine. The first
picture represents the ordination of St. Stephen by St.
Peter, and is probably by a pupil of Juanes. The other

paintings are by the master's hand. In these, we see the
saint with the face of an angel, meeting the scornful brows
of priest and doctor. They listen silent ; then the uproar
begins, and he turns on them with a bold rebuke. They
hear no more ; they rise on him, they drag him forth, a
mob of angry rabbis to his doom. The contrast of the
calm dignity of Saul, the rapt face of the saint, with the
exultant rage of the mob, is finely drawn. With bowed
knees the martyr receives his crown; with a last look,
whether it were a heavenly vision, or the rapt eye of faith,
he sees the Son of God, and with one prayer he " falls
asleep." The last in the series, the " Burial of Stephen,"
is very beautiful. No. 755, " The Last Supper," painted
for the Church of San Estebano, at Valencia, is a noble
and characteristic example of Juanes. The head of Judas
is powerfully drawn, and those of some of the other apostles are fine. With all Juanes' wealth of colour, it has little of his usual hard outline. In Nos. 761 and 762, the
figures of Aaron and Melchisedec stand out from the
canvas as if in flesh and blood. Juanes was a portrait-
painter of keenest eye and nicest hand. No. 754, the
portrait of Don Luis de Castelvi is one of his finest works.
Don Luis stands before us, no shadow but a living man,
a courtier of the time of Charles V., with the cross of
Santiago on his breast, and a small book in his uplifted
right hand.

But it is in Valencia that Juanes must be studied. In
the museum are only five of his paintings, but in the

cathedral and other churches there still remain many of his finest works. Of these are a "Last Supper" in the Church of St. Nicolas, and several smaller paintings ; and in the sacristy of the cathedral is a "Good Shepherd Bearing a Lamb."

Juanes left a son, Juan Vicente Juanes, also a painter, and an imitator of his father's style.

21. THE ESCURIAL.

IV.

THE Escorial is the one monument of the age of Philip II. which is left in the modern world of Madrid. There can be nothing at once more disappointing, nor yet more striking. It stands, about three hours' ride from the city, amidst the cold, bare mountains, a huge pile of granite; monastery and church together. The exterior is a clumsy mass with a central dome, surrounded by a dull garden, and within a gloomy church, cloisters, and apartments where the king spent his last years. His apartments were a small square room, with brick floor, and two smaller alcoves for his cot-bed and writing-table. Below was the Pantheon, the tomb of the Spanish kings and queens. It seems the very type of the narrow and gloomy religion that overshadowed him, the living sepulchre of this Christian Pharaoh.

In this character lies the root of Spanish institutions and social habits—institutions and habits which existed nowhere else over the breadth of the continent. The theory of race in this day has been made the great solvent of history. But if Spanish art owes much of its distinctive character to its local insulation, it owes yet more

43

to the tenacity of the Roman root which struck with more vigour into the soil of the Iberian Peninsula than into that of the Italian, and gained a development that was elsewhere denied to it. It is only as we study the growth of the Papal power that we can understand Spanish art. Over every individual, in his civic and social ways, the Church exercised the strictest espionage. It enacted the stringent laws which have come down to us as monuments at once of the piety and the asceticism of the past. It was, in the eyes of the Holy Inquisition, a special privilege which God had given them to work out this problem of repression in a world of corrupt systems and habits. Their work had at once the loftiness and the narrowness of this idea, it cherished the virtues of private morality in a day of Papal corruption, but it cherished also the most gloomy asceticism, which gave to all art a religious cast. Even when it had lost its living faith, a stern fanaticism that still observed the letter of the law filled them with horror for the artist's study of the human form, whether directly from nature or from the antique. The Spanish painter was not commonly a man of bad morals, but rather we suppose him of strict and laborious habits, and a man who dwelt in the frozen zone of a spiritual pride. In his art he had but one thought—the maintenance and illustration of his religious traditions; he had scant visions of ideal beauty, and little accurate knowledge of the human form. We admire the grandeur of fanaticism itself · but we feel that it palsies art. It makes of its dogmas iron yokes to be riveted by force. At least the outward man shall be calm and passionless—a volcano covered at the top with snows,—even though the consuming fires of the heart are burning below. It is this thraldom which has narrowed Spanish art.

A life-like sketch of the workings of the Inquisition may be found in Pacheco's "Arte de la Pintura." He begins with an assurance of his fitness as a censor of sacred pictures. "My remarks will serve as salutory counsel, offered as they are at the age of seventy ; all that is best and most assured in them is principally owing to the sacred religion of the company of Jesus, which has perfected them. I find myself at this moment rich in hints and observations, the result of the advice and approval of the wisest men since the year 1605. It will not, therefore, appear alien from my profession to point out to Christian painters the methods which they ought to pursue, more especially since I find myself honoured with a particular commission from the holy tribunal of the Inquisition, to denounce the errors committed in pictures of this class by the ignorance or wickedness of artists. This commission was made out and sealed on the 7th of March, 1618: a part of it runs as follows : ' In consideration of our regard for the person of Francisco Pacheco, inhabitant of this city, an excellent painter, and brother of Juan Perez Pacheco, Familiar of this Holy Office, and having regard to his wisdom and prudence,—we give him commission, and charge him henceforward, that he

take particular care to inspect and visit the paintings of
sacred subjects which may stand in shops or in public
places.'   It then goes on to say that if I find any thing to
object to in them, I am to take the picture before My
Lords the Inquisitors, in order that they, having seen
them, may take such order as may be fitting therein ; and
it concludes with the words—' and for this end we give
him commission such as is of right required.' " [1]

In the " Last Judgment " of Michael Angelo, Pacheco is
not only shocked by so many naked figures, but he
severely censures other things. " As to placing the
damned in the air, fighting as they are with one another,
and pulling against the devils, when it is a matter of faith
that they must want the free gifts of glory, and cannot,
therefore, possess the requisite lightness or agility—the
impropriety of this mode of exhibiting them is self evident.   With regard, again, to the angels without wings
and the saints without clothes, although the former do not
possess the one and the latter will not have the other, yet
since angels without wings are not known to us, and our
eyes do not allow us to see the saints without clothes,
as we shall hereafter, there can be no doubt that this again
is improper." [2]

Pacheco finds it hard to reconcile his duty as Inspector
of the Inquisition with his knowledge as artist, in the
question of study from life.   " I seem," he says, " to hear

---

[1] Head, p. 9.
[2] Head, p. 10.

some one asking me: 'Señor Painter, scrupulous as you
are, whilst you place before us as examples the ancient
artists who contemplated the figures of naked women in
order to imitate them perfectly, and while you charge us
to paint well, what resource do you afford us?' I would
answer : 'Señor Licentiate, this is what I would do; I
would paint the faces and hands from nature, with the
requisite beauty and variety, after women of good character ; in which, in my opinion, there is no danger. With
regard to the other parts, I would avail myself of good
pictures, engravings, drawings, models, ancient and
modern statues, and the excellent designs of Albrecht
Dürer; so that I might choose what was most graceful
and best composed without running into danger.'"[1]

To illustrate the danger of immodest pictures, Pacheco
tells the story of a good bishop who had been to America,
and who said that he would rather face a hurricane in the
Gulf of Bermuda than officiate again opposite a certain
altar-piece, the "Last Judgment," by Martin de Vos, in
the Augustine convent at Seville.

Carducho tells how a certain painter was cast into the
flames of Purgatory for having painted a *pintura des-
honesta*, as all representations of the nude were termed.
He appeared to his confessor and prayed him to beseech
the owner of the picture to burn it, that he might enter
Paradise. Then follows the general maxim, that *pintar
cosas deshonestas es pecado mortal.* Later on Carducho

---

[1] Head, p. 11.

mentions that among the pictures presented to the Prince of Wales (Charles I.) was an "Antiope" by Titian, which was one of the few paintings saved when the royal palace of the Pardo was burned in 1604. Many magnificent works perished; but this, with all its profanity, could escape the fire ("*y estar con ser tan profana, pudo escapar dal fuego*").

The Inquisition enforced upon the painter a rigid penance in all cases of impropriety in costume; as in the case of an artist at Cordova who painted "our Lady at the foot of the cross with a *verdugado* (that is, a hooped petticoat, close at the hips and gradually widening), 'with a *jubon de puntas*' (perhaps a pointed bodice), 'and with a saffron-coloured head-dress'; St. John had '*calzas atacadas*' (pantaloons) and a '*jubon con agujetas*' (doublet with points). Another painter, in his 'Marriage of the Virgin,' represented her without any mantle, in a Venetian petticoat, fitting very close in the waist, covered with knots of coloured ribbon, and with wide, round sleeves ('*mangas grandes de ruldas*'), a dress," our author adds, "in my opinion very unbecoming the dignity of this our Sovereign Lady."[1]

"Pacheco says: 'What can be more foreign from the respect which we owe to the purity of Our Lady the Virgin than to paint her sitting down, with one of her knees placed over the other, and often with her sacred feet uncovered and naked? (Let thanks be given to the

---

[1] Head, p. 13.

Holy Inquisition, which commands that this liberty should be corrected.) We scarcely ever, therefore, in Spanish pictures see the feet of the Virgin. Carducho speaks more particularly on the impropriety of painting the Virgin unshod, since it is manifest that Our Lady was in the habit of wearing shoes, as is proved by 'the much venerated relic of one of them from her divine feet in the Cathedral of Burgos.'"[1] There is a charming *naïveté* in this logic of the pious Carducho.

Exact rules were laid down for painting the different periods of the Virgin's life, even to the minutest detail of age, costume, and posture. In the pictures of the conception Pacheco says: "In this gracefulest of mysteries Our Lady is to be pourtrayed in the bloom of youth, from twelve to thirteen years old, with sweet, grave eyes, a nose and mouth of perfect form, rosy cheeks, and fair golden hair hanging loosely,—in a word, with all the beauty that a human pencil can depict." At her feet is to be a crescent with horns pointing downward; the twelve stars above are raised on silver rays; the sun is represented by a bright golden light behind the figure,— she bears the form of the vision in the Apocalypse of the " woman clothed with the sun and the moon under her feet, and having upon her head a crown of twelve stars." Her robe is white, and her mantle blue; and she wears the cord of St. Francis, because thus she appeared to Beatriz de Silva, a noble nun of Portugal, who founded in 1511 a religious order of the Conception at Toledo.

---

[1] Head, p. 14.

Pacheco is much troubled ("*causa me gran compas-sion*") at seeing the infant Jesus represented naked in his mother's arms. St. Joseph, he says, had an office, and was well off; it was not possible, therefore, that his child should have been without the bare necessities which the meanest beggar can afford. Ayala, in " El Pintor Chris-tiano y Erudito," devotes several pages to finding fault with such painters as drew the cross like a T, instead of in the usual Latin form, †; and he argues the all-important question as to whether two angels or only one shall be seated on the stone in pictures of the " Maries at the Sep-ulchre "; he decides that it will be well to alternate the two methods. He debates, too, the propriety of giving horns and tail to the Devil, and decides that Santa Teresa's vision authorizes the use of the former, and that, although not strictly proven, still he probably had a tail.

These are but a few of the swaddling clothes which the Church bound around all art, until we wonder that there was any originality or capacity of growth left in Spain. They must grievously have fettered all artists. That these restrictions were sometimes ignored we learn from a contract entered into with El Mudo by the authorities of the Escorial, wherein it is expressly stipulated that "wherever the figure of a saint is repeated by painting it several times, the face shall be represented in the same manner, and likewise the garments shall be of the same colour; and if any saint has a portrait which is peculiar to him, he shall be painted according to said portrait, which

shall be sought out with diligence, wherever it may be ;
and in the aforesaid pictures the artist shall not introduce
any cat or dog or other unbecoming figure, but all shall
be saints ; and such as incite to devotion." [1]

This stipulation was made because not long before that
Navarrete had placed a partridge, and a dog and a cat
quarrelling, in a picture of the Holy Trinity.

We now come to one of the greatest painters among
the great contributors to the treasure-house of the Escorial. Juan Fernandez Navarrete, *El Mudo*, was born at
Logroño in 1526. When he was but three years old a
severe illness destroyed his sense of hearing. He soon
learned, however, to make known all his wants by the
only language he ever mastered—the artist's tongue—a
bit of charcoal. On discovering his great talent Fray
Vicente, in the Monastery of Estrella, became his teacher,
and afterward sent him to Italy ; where he, perhaps,
studied awhile under Titian at Venice. He was recalled
to Spain, and in 1568, appointed painter to the king, by
whom he was employed at the Escorial.

His picture of the "Baptism of Christ," formerly in
the *celda prioral* at the Escorial, now in the Prado (No.
905), was executed at this time for a specimen of the
painter's ability—it is the only specimen of Navarrete's
purely Florentine manner. The Prado possesses also
two noble figures of St. Paul (Nos. 906, 907). But it is in
the Escorial that El Mudo has left the great impress of

his genius. A number of the minor altars and the piers were executed by this artist, "who spoke by his pencil with the bravura of Rubens, without his coarseness, and with a richness of colour often rivalling Titian." The noblest of these paintings, which represent the apostles and saints, are the figures of St. Philip, St. Andrew, and St. James. Besides these in the upper cloisters are a "St. Jerome," a "Christ Appearing to his Mother after his Resurrection," an "Adoration of Shepherds," and a "Nativity." In the latter Navarrete has employed three different lights—coming from the child, the glory above, and a candle held by St. Joseph. The figures of the shepherds are nobly treated. Tibaldi Pellegrino always exclaimed when he looked at the picture, "*O ! gli belli pastori.*" "The grand picture of Abraham and the Angels, now in the collection of the Duke of Dalmatia, was also originally in the Escorial. The effect of the whole is very peculiar; the angel at the right is fine, and the light falling on the feet of the three figures, with the rich glow of colour on the bending form of Abraham, is grand and most remarkable. Pacheco thinks the subject is treated indecorously, because the angels are represented *con ropas moradas Nazareñas,* when they ought to have been painted as pilgrims; above all, he is shocked at their having beards." [1]

El Mudo, says Cean Bermudez, was a man of unusual talent; and in no ordinary degree versed in sacred and

---

[1] Head, p. 78.

profane history and in mythology. He read and wrote, and played cards, speaking always by signs, but with such clear and concise expression that it roused the admiration of all who talked with him. When Titian's magnificent picture of the "Last Supper" reached the Escorial it was too large for its intended position in the Refectory. El Mudo was very indignant when the king ordered it to be cut down to the required size; he offered, expressing himself by signs, to make an exact copy of it in six months, and this at the risk of his head; then making the sign of the cross on his breast he said that he should deserve the order of knighthood, if in six months he accomplished what had taken Titian seven years to achieve. Philip had not patience enough to wait for a copy, and to Navarrete's great sorrow the noble work was cut down to the needful size.

Navarrete died at Toledo in 1572, having finished only eight of the twenty-two saints and evangelists which he had agreed to paint for the Escorial. The work was completed by Sanchez Coello and Carbarajal.

Lope de Vega, in the " Laurel de Apolo," laments over Navarrete's death, whom he calls the Spanish painter who best rivals the Italian masters. Of his work he says:

> Ningun rostro pinto que fuese mudo—
> No face he painted that was dumb.

Navarrete founded no school of painting; and yet as the first follower of the Venetian manner, his influence on

Spanish art was very great. His bold design, his noble
wealth of colour, his broad and free handling, combined
with a thorough mastery of the chiaro-scuro and a wonderful use of varied lights, made him a true forerunner of the
great masters.

According to Cean Bermudez, Alonso Sanchez Coello
was born at Benifayro, in Valencia, early in the sixteenth
century. His early style is a peculiar blending of the
Flemish and Italian manners, one that we often meet
among the artists of his day; as, for instance, in Frans
Floris, Martin de Vos, or Michael Coxis. In 1542 Sanchez Coello entered the studio of Antonio Moro, then at
Madrid; whose influence on his later work is very marked.
Sanchez Coello's colour and treatment, especially in his
portraits, approach very closely the manner of Moro.

In 1543 Sanchez Coello went with Moro to Portugal,
where he was employed by the Infant Don Juan; at the
death of that prince he entered the service of Philip II.,
who made him his painter in ordinary. The king distinguished him most highly, often visiting him at his work
in the studio, which was in the palace; writing to him as
"his beloved son Alonso Sanchez Coello, and treating him
with an extreme and uniform kindness. Sanchez Coello
amassed a large fortune, having many patrons besides the
king. " 'Seventeen royal personages,' says Palomino,
'honoured him with their esteem, and would sometimes
recreate and refresh themselves under his roof, with his
wife and children.'" At his death in 1590, according to

Palomino, the seventy-fifth year of his age, he left a fortune of 55,000 ducats, part of which went to endow an hospital for orphans at Valladolid.

"An anecdote related by Porreño, the biographer of Philip II., shows how high the artist stood in the estimation of the court. Don Diego de Cordoba, chancing to see exposed for sale some wretched portraits of the king, in a fit of loyal indignation rushed into the royal presence, and besought his majesty to follow the example of Alexander the Great, and to 'grant to Alonso Sanchez, or some other famous painter,' the exclusive right of depicting his gracious countenance. 'Let the poor daubsters live,' said the king, 'so long as they misrepresent our faces, and not our behaviour.'"[1] He painted some historical pictures, most of which perished in the fires at the Pardo, a royal sitio or shooting-box six miles from the city, and the palace at Madrid. In 1582 he executed several altar-pieces for the Church of the Escorial, and a portrait of the Padre Siguenza for the *celda prioral.* The saints that he painted at the Escorial are noble; above all San Ignazio, a wonderfully powerful and striking figure. In the Prado are ten of his works, among which is the "Marriage of St. Catharine," painted on cork. But it is as a portrait-painter that Sanchez Coello won and kept his fame. Philip was often pourtrayed by his favourite; although the Prado does not possess one of his portraits. The portraits of Don Carlos and the Infanta

---

[1] Stirling-Maxwell, p. 234.

Isabel Clara Eugenia (Nos. 1032, 1033) are fine compositions, recalling forcibly the style of Antonio Moro.

Of the school of Sanchez Coello were his daughter Doña Isabella, a fine musician as well as an excellent artist; Cristobal Lopez, Felipe de Liano, Juan da Urbino, Giovanni Narducci, and the most famous of his scholars— Pantoja de la Cruz.

Pantoja was born at Madrid in 1551. After leaving the studio of Sanchez Coello he was appointed painter to the king and *ayuda de camara* (gentleman of the chamber). He was an admirable portrait-painter, and excelled in his pictures of animals. An anecdote in this connection is given by Francisco Velez de Arciniega, in his work on Natural History. The king employed Pantoja to paint a bearded eagle which one of his fowlers had caught in the royal chase near the Prado. Pantoja seized with such skill the life-like expression of the bird, that, getting loose, it dashed at the canvas and tore it to pieces; the picture had to be painted again. Arciniega saw the eagle afterward in the hospital of Anton Martin, at Madrid; he was of reddish-black colour, and had "a grave and composed manner of gazing, which showed no little grandeur and authority." Pantoja executed numerous works for the churches and convents of Madrid. Many of his pictures have perished in the fires at the royal palaces. His works show truth and purity of design, warmth and transparency of colour, and careful finish in detail. In the Prado are twelve paintings by Pantoja; two of which—the "Birth

of the Virgin," and the "Nativity "—are of special interest, as they contain certain portraits of the family of
Philip III. "In the former, St. Anne is dimly seen reclining in a state bed with crimson hangings; in the foreground stands a graceful damsel bathing the new-born
babe. In the latter, the Virgin has the features of Queen
Margaret, and the Austrian lip and hanging cheek may be
detected in several of the surrounding shepherds and
peasant girls. Both pictures are signed :

JVAN PANTOJA DE LA †, 1603."[1]

The exact date of Pantoja's death is not known, but it
occurred before 1609, as Lope de Vega, in his " Jerusalem
Conquistada," published in that year, laments for the
painter.

Luis de Carbarajal, or Carbajal, born at Toledo in 1534,
was employed at the. Escorial in completing the work begun by Navarrete. Later in life he was associated with
Blas del Prado in certain work at Toledo, where, too, he
painted a portrait of Don Bartolomé Carranza, for the
Winter Chapter-House. In the Prado is a " Magdalen "
by this artist.

Blas del Prado was also a native of Toledo ; he was
probably a scholar of Francisco Comontes. He painted,
in 1591, a " Holy Family " for the *Geronimos* at Guadalupe ; and for the *Franciscanos* at Toledo, in connection
with Carbajal, he executed a *retablo* with St. Blas and
other saints; also a " Descent from the Cross," for the

[1] Stirling-Maxwell, pp. 268, 269.

Church of San Pedro at Madrid. In the Prado is a fine painting by del Prado, representing the Virgin and Child enthroned. St. Joseph stands by them, while below kneels Alfonso de Villegas, the historian of the calendar; they are attended by St. John and St. Ildefonso. This picture is executed in a noble Florentine manner, with fine tone and careful drapery; in some points it recalls Fra Bartolommeo.

In 1593, the Emperor of Morocco requested Philip II. to send him a painter. The king replied that they had in Spain two kinds of painters, the ordinary and the excellent, and wished to know which the emperor desired. " Kings should always have the best," was the proud Moor's answer; and accordingly Blas del Prado was sent to Fez. He painted a portrait of the emperor's daughter, and executed sundry works in the palace to the monarch's entire satisfaction. After passing several years in Morocco the painter returned to Castile, laden with the generous gifts of the Moorish prince. Del Prado is said to have adopted the Moorish dress and many Oriental customs, as, for instance, eating in the Eastern fashion, reclining amongst cushions. He died probably about 1600.

Luis de Velasco was associated with Blas del Prado in 1591 in painting a *retablo* for the Franciscan convent. In 1584 he was employed by the Chapter of Toledo: over the door of the church is his fine Incarnation, and in the cloister a " Virgin and Child," with St. Anthony, St. Blas,

and an armed knight, the Infante Don Fernando, with
two saints. Velasco was an able painter, with an accurate and pleasing colour; his works show a fair knowledge
of antique sculpture and the best Italian art. He died
in 1606.

We now come to the name of Domenico Theotocupuli,
El Greco, a painter of undoubted genius, but of an order
of genius that often mistook the grotesque for the sublime, the bold for the lofty, the novel for the creative.
Palomino said of him: *Lo que hizó bien ninguno lo hizó
mejor, y lo que hizó mal ninguno lo hizó peor.* (What he
did well none could do better, and what he did ill none
could do worse.)

We know nothing of El Greco's earlier history. Our
first authentic record is that in 1577 he was living at
Toledo, where he painted the fine picture of the "Stripping of Christ" in the sacristy of the cathedral; he also
executed the carving and ornament of this *retablo.* "The
figure of Christ is in the centre, clothed in deep crimson,
and from its position and the glow of its colour, as well as
the grouping of the subordinate personages, gives an unity
to this work which has been rarely surpassed. The tone
is essentially Venetian." [1] This is the finest example of
El Greco's early manner; in its careful drawing, transparent warmth of colour, and grandeur of composition it is
worthy of a follower of Titian. Pacheco tells us: "When
I asked Domenico Greco, in 1611, which was the more

---

[1] Head, p. 81.

difficult, drawing or colour," his answer was colour ; and
this opinion of his is not so much to be wondered at as
to hear him talk with so little esteem for Michael Angelo
(being, as he is, the father of painting), of whom he said
that " he was a good sort of man (*buen ombre*), but did not
know how to paint."

Two years later El Greco painted the " Martyrdom of
San Mauricio " for the Escorial. In this he abandoned
entirely the Venetian manner ; adopting a hard and dry
colour, with strange, weird gleams of light everywhere'
vigorous, and striking figures, but of a severe, realistic
type and exaggerated expression, and throughout a dry,
grey, spotted tone : yet the heads are admirable ; they
stand forth from the canvas with marvellous power, a
strange medley of the sublime and the grotesque.

This picture little pleased the king, and, while paid for,
it was hung in a chapel of the Colegio instead of being
placed in the church. But El Greco's masterpiece is the
" Burial of the Count of Orgaz," painted for the Church
of Santo Tomas at Toledo. It is a noble painting, rich
in colour, each figure real, though lacking in the broad
Venetian treatment of the " Stripping of Christ." It is a
characteristic example of El Greco's best manner. St.
Stephen and St. Augustin descend to earth that they
may bury the noble Count Gonzalo Ruiz. The contrast of
the youthful beauty of Stephen with the venerable figure
of St. Augustin, and the calm grandeur of the dead warrior as they lower him to the grave, are very fine. To the

right of the picture kneels a fair-haired boy, behind him a group of priests with lighted tapers, while in the background stand the friends and family, probably all portraits. The upper part of the picture is disappointing. It represents the entrance of the departed soul into paradise. It is sadly lacking in colour and symmetry.

El Greco was an architect and sculptor as well as painter. From his designs were built the Chapel of the Franciscan College at Madrid, the Ayuntamiento at Toledo, and the two churches of the Caridad and the Franciscans at Llescas. The latter were decorated with carvings and paintings by his own hand. In the Prado are ten works of El Greco, nine of them portraits. The finest are No. 241, Don Rodrigo Vasquez, President of Castile; and No. 242, a "dark, handsome man in armour with a curious chain of gold and tricolour silk around his neck—which Velasquez never excelled." At Toledo in the Museum of San Juan de los Reyes, is El Greco's fine portrait of Juan de Alava; and in the Hospital of San Juan Bautista, the portrait of Cardinal Tavera. Here is also a charming "Holy Family," and in the sacristy of the cathedral a "Christ bearing the Cross," by the same artist.

El Greco died in 1625; there are few in that day who exercised such influence on Spanish art; he is the first of the ascetic, realistic school, the school of Zurbaran and Ribera and Valdes Leal.

Among his pupils was Fray Juan Bautista Mayno, a

Dominican monk, employed by the Toledan Chapter to fresco the cloisters and to paint several altar-pieces. He was also drawing-master to the heir apparent—later Philip IV., during whose reign he had general direction of all art matters. It was by Mayno that Alonso Cano was brought to the king's notice. The only work of this artist in the Prado is an allegorical painting, No. 787, representing the reduction of a revolted province in Flanders, and containing portraits of Philip IV. and of Olivarez.

Chief among El Greco's pupils was Luis Tristan, born near Toledo in 1526. He was an apt scholar, and a favourite with his master, who often gave him commissions that he himself could not undertake. There is a well-known anecdote told of a picture of the "Last Supper," which Tristan executed for the Hieronymite Monastery of La Sisla. The picture pleased the monks, but not so the price of two hundred ducats; they therefore sent to El Greco, asking him to fix its value. On seeing the picture the master rushed toward Tristan with uplifted stick, berating him as a rascal and a disgrace to his calling. The monks remonstrated; the lad, they said, was ignorant, but very willing to submit to his master's verdict. "Forsooth," exclaimed El Greco, "he *is* ignorant, "the picture is worth five hundred, not two hundred ducats. Roll it up and take it to my house." The monks now gladly paid the artist's price without further haggling. About 1616 Tristan painted his masterpiece, a series of pictures

for the Church of Yepes. They represent the "Adoration of the Shepherds," the "Adoration of the Kings,"
"Christ at the Column," "Christ Bearing the Cross," the
"Resurrection," the "Ascension," and several figures of
saints. The finest portrait by Tristan is that of Cardinal
de Sandoval, Archbishop of Toledo. About the same
time he painted the poet Lope de Vega; this portrait is
now in the Hermitage. There is but one picture by Tristan in the Prado—a striking portrait of an old man with
a stick in his hand. At the Academy is a powerful St.
Jerome, which recalls Titian.

Tristan united a correct drawing with the rich colour and
bold, free handling of his master's best manner; without
the extravagant lights and shadows and the unnatural
flesh-tints that El Greco sometimes used. He was well
worthy to be the master of Velazquez.

Among the many foreign artists who flocked to Spain
at Philip's bidding, and whose work is embalmed in the
Escorial, are Antonio and Vincenzio Campi, of Cremona;
Luca Cambiaso, of Genoa, his son Horazio, and his pupil Lazzaro Taverone; Juan Bautista Castello surnamed
"el Bergamasco," Romulo Cincinato, and Patricio Caxes.
Better known is Federigo Zuccaro, who came to Spain
to work at the Escorial; but failing to please the king,
he returned soon to Italy. Pellegrino Tibaldi was employed to replace much of Zuccaro's work—among others,
"A Martyrdom of St. Lawrence," a "Nativity," and an
"Adoration of Kings" for the high altar. "The pictures

in the *retablo* of the Adoration and Nativity are very
cold; while his San Lorenzo '*non satis crematus*,' puts
out the fire for very rawness. Again, the martyr is so
gigantic, that he might have eaten up the disproportionate
Romans as easily as Captain Gulliver routed the Lilli-
putians."[1]   The Caracci called him *il Michelagnolo ri-
formato;* but he was a Michael Angelo without his
grandeur or originality; his paintings were to Michael
Angelo's what the ravings of Bedlam are to an opera of
Gounod.   One of his most successful works was the fresco
of the library ceiling at the Escorial, on which he represented in allegory the "liberal arts,"—Philosophy, Gram-
mar, Rhetoric, Dialectic, Arithmetic, Music, Geometry,
Astronomy, and Theology.   Bartolomé Carducho (born in
Florence, 1560) was chosen to decorate the frieze of the
library.   This he did with marvellous power, following out
Pellegrini's allegory most happily.   Thus, beneath Arithmetic, he represented Solomon solving a problem given
him by the Queen of Sheba; and the power of Eloquence
was symbolized by a Hercules, from whose mouth came
chains of gold to bind the nations.   Carducho's finest
works in oil were those executed for the Church of San
Felipe el Real, which were all destroyed in the fire of
1718, save a "Descent from the Cross," now at the Prado.
It has a simple purity of design, not without grandeur
but is cold and hard in colour.   In the Prado are also a
"Last Supper," and a "Martyrdom of St. Sebastian," by

[1] Ford, p. 813.

Carducho. He executed several works, both in fresco and oil, in the church of San Andres, at Valladolid. His works are carefully finished, touched and retouched repeatedly; his aim, as he himself expressed it, was to be judged by those acquainted with art, not by the vulgar herd. "Prudence and disinterestedness were," Cean Bermudez says, "his peculiar virtues." He was one day admiring a newly finished picture by an artist friend of his, when one of his own pupils called his attention to a poorly-drawn and ill-placed foot. "I did not notice it," answered the painter, "it is so hidden by the difficult excellence of this bosom and those hands."

Carducho died in 1608. Among his pupils were Francisco Lopez, Juan de Soto, and Vicente Carducho,—his younger brother,—the author of the "Dialogos sobre la Pintura."

Vicente Carducho was born at Florence, in 1578. At the age of seven years he came with his brother Bartolomé to Madrid. He says of himself : " My native country is the most noble city of Florence ; but as I have been educated from my early years in Spain, and at the court of our Catholic monarchs, who have honoured me with royal favours, I may truly consider myself a native of Madrid." Educated in Bartolomé's studio, Vicente's early manner resembles closely that of his brother; he afterward adopted more the style of the Spanish *Naturalisti*. At his brother's death he was appointed, in his place, painter to the king, to finish some work for the royal *sitio* of the Pardo. In 1615, associated with Eugenio Caxes, he completed the fresco in "Our Lady of the Sanctuary," in the Cathedral at Toledo ; and, in 1618, he executed six paintings for the *Geronimos* at Guadalupe: the "Annunciation," the "Nativity," "Assumption of the Virgin," and the "Pentecost." Vicente's rapid pencil has left its traces on many of the churches and convents of Madrid ; with all the ravages of time there yet remains enough to prove his admirable skill and pure, noble design. In the Prado are eight of his pictures. His greatest work, now in the *Musco Nacional* at Madrid, is a series of fifty-four pictures painted for the Carthusian monastery of Paular on the Guadarama. Twenty-six of these paintings represent scenes from the life of St. Bruno.

The others depict the sufferings of the order. "The two compositions on the death of Bruno are full of grace and feeling and abound in noble heads. Amongst the works which treat of his followers, three very striking pictures represent the sufferings of the English Carthusians at our Reformation. In two of these, the scene is a prison, where, chained to the pillars, emaciated monks lie dead or dying in their white robes, and open doors give a distant view of fierce Protestant tormentors. In a third, three Carthusians are hurried off to execution on a hurdle, dragged by horses, which are urged to full speed by their rider, and likewise diligently lashed by a man who runs by the side, the "*Adelantaro*," or "forwarder," of a Spanish stage-coach at the present day; some spectators look gaily on, and seem to point exultingly at the gallows and ladder in the distance. Occasionally, in the series, the blessed Virgin appears, to comfort some holy man, and to relieve the monotony of some male and monkish figures. In one of these cases the Mother of Mercy chases from the cell of a sleeping Carthusian a band of demons, of which, one giant monster, with a bull's head and the mouth of a dragon, stalks away on a pair of satyr's legs, poising a hooked spear on his shoulder, and the rest flit forth in the shape of unclean birds, or untwine themselves from the bedposts in the likeness of serpents breathing flames.

" Like many other trophies of Spanish art, these fine works of Carducho have lost much of their significance by removal from the spot for which they were painted. Hung on the crowded walls of an ill-ordered museum, his Carthusian histories can never again speak to the heart and the fancy as they once spoke in the lonely cloister of Paular, where the silence was only broken by the breeze as it moaned through the overhanging pine forest, by the tinkling bell, or the choral chant of the chapel, or by the stealing tread of some mute and white-stoled monk, the brother and the heir of the holy men of old, whose good deeds and sufferings were there commemorated on canvas. There, to many generations of recluses, vowed to perpetual silence and solitude, these pictures had been companions; to them the painted saints and martyrs had become friends. In the Chartreuse, therefore, absurdities were veiled, or criticism awed, by the venerable genius of the place; while in the Museum, the monstrous legend and extravagant picture, stripped of every illusion, are coolly judged of on their own merits as works of skill and imagination. Still, notwithstanding their present disadvantages of position, these pictures vindicate the high fame of Carducho, and will bear comparison with the best history ever painted of the Carthusian order. Less elegant, perhaps, than the paintings that were executed twenty years later by Eustache Le Sueur for the Chartreuse of Paris, Carducho's works far excel these in vigour of style, variety of fancy, and richness of colour; draperies grander than his are hardly to be found in the monastic studies of Zurbaran; and few Castilian masters have ever rivalled the pensive and delicate beauty of his Madonnas. These pictures are, for the most part, signed Vin. Carduchi, P. R. F. (*i. e.*, Pictor Regis Fecit)." [1]

In 1633, Carducho published his "*Dialogos sobre la Pintura*," which Cean Bermudez thinks the best work of its kind in Spanish.

Carducho died at Madrid in 1638, and was buried in the chapel of San Francisco.

Of his school were Felix Castello, Francisco Fernandez, Pedro de Obregon, Bartolomé Roman, Francisco Rizi, and Francisco Collantes.

---

[1] Stirling-Maxwell, pp. 420, 421, 422.

V.

THE SCHOOLS OF VALENCIA AND SEVILLE.

AFTER Juanes, the first of the great painters of the Valencian school is Francisco Ribalta, who was born at Castellon de la Plana, about 1551. He studied first at Valencia under an unknown painter, probably a follower of Juanes. We are told that he fell in love with his master's daughter, and asked her hand in marriage. On the father's refusal he went to Italy, having won the maiden's promise to wait for him. There he studied the works of Raffaelle and Sebastian del Piombo; and was probably awhile at Bologna with the Carracci.

On his return to Valencia, Ribalta hastened to his master's house; and, finding him absent, seized a brush and palette, completed a sketch that lay on an easel, and departed. When the painter came home and found the finished picture, calling his daughter to him he exclaimed: "This is the artist I would have thee marry, and not that daubster Ribalta." It is needless to say that the marriage took place shortly afterward.

Ribalta's earliest work at Valencia is a portrait, now in England, of his wife and himself. It shows clearly his Italian study.

Ribalta is only to be understood in Valencia. In the Museum are eight fine paintings, but the *Colegio de Corpus* is the true museum of this master. His favourite subject was the life of San Vicente de Ferrer. In one of the chapels of Corpus Christi is his masterpiece: "San Vicente de Ferrer visited on his sick-bed by the Saviour and Saints"; and over the high altar hangs a "Last Supper." "The general effect of the picture, with its rich red and blue draperies, is very grand; and the heads are, most of them, carefully painted from fine models,—that of St. John, contrary to custom, being the least beautiful of them all [1]; the head of an Apostle, with a white beard, is equal to any thing painted by the old Venetians; the Judas in the foreground is said to be the portrait of a shoemaker by whom Ribalta was worried."[2] Over the "Last Supper" hangs a charming "Holy Family," and in the library is a noble "Christ at the Column," in the manner of Sebastian del Piombo; and a fine "Christ in the Garden of Olives."

In the Prado are four fine specimens of Ribalta. The "St. Francis of Assisi, on his pallet, listening to an angel playing on the lute," is one of the finest. It is rich in colour, and the figure of the saint noble and well drawn; but the angel is wanting in life and expression. There is also a grand head with a most agonized expression, representing a soul in torment; its companion-piece is a soul

---

[1] Stirling-Maxwell, p. 492.
[2] Ford, I, p. 444.

in paradise. The "Dead Christ in the Arms of Two Angels," No. 946, is executed in a noble Italian manner, and shows an excellent knowledge of anatomy, a correct modelling, careful drapery, and rich colour. The angels are very beautiful.

Ribalta died in 1628. A patient, untiring artist, he left many admirable works. But every one familiar with Italian art must recognize in him an imitator of it. This is really his secret, as it is the secret of so many Spanish painters: that he introduced Italian art, the growth of a foreign soil, into Catholic Spain. Its noble traditions, its fine sentiment, and rich colour are his. As we look on his canvas, we are reminded, now of Juanes, now of Sebastian del Piombo, now of Domenichino, and the Carracci; yet he is not a plagiarist, a gem-stealer, but he has caught their style and continued it, as the disciples of Raffaelle sometimes finished parts of his pictures, and, therefore, his influence passed away; he founded no great school; he left no pupils to carry on his traditions ; he marked no epoch in art as did a Navarrete or a Tristan ; he accepted it as it was.

The most noted of Ribalta's pupils were Ribera, who soon left him for the robust school of Caravaggio ; Gregorio Bausa; Castaneda, who was also his son-in-law ; and Juan de Ribalta, born in 1597, a worthy follower of his father. His paintings resemble so closely those of Francisco that until very recently they were often confounded. In the *Museo* at Valencia is a fine Crucifixion painted when Juan was but nineteen years old: it was executed for the Convent of San Miguel de los Reyes. "The composition, which is of necessity crowded with soldiers, priests, and rabble, is managed with great skill ; the moment chosen by the artist is that of the elevation of the cross. The foreshortened figure of our Lord is admirably painted; and in his noble countenance the struggle is finely expressed between the agony of the suffering man and the resignation of the self-sacrificing God. To the left, stands one of the thieves awaiting his turn, with his hands tied behind him, and his face turned away, his broad shoulders affording an excellent study of anatomy; and a brawny executioner, in the foreground, stooping down to bore a hole in the plank, is designed and coloured in the bold manner of Rubens. These rude figures are well contrasted by the sorrowing group behind, the Virgin, Mary Magdalene, St. John, and their company." [1]

Juan de Ribalta died in the same year as his father, in 1628.

Pedro Orrente was born at Monte Alegre in Murcia in the latter half of the sixteenth century. His early style resembles that of Tristan and Mayno, and he probably studied with El Greco at Toledo. His pictures show a broad and free handling with rich colour in the Venetian manner. His masterpiece is his St. Sebastian in the cathedral at Valencia. In many of his works he

---

[1] Stirling-Maxwell, p. 497.

recalls Bassano ; and shows great power in the grouping of his animals. Some of the best of these are the "Adoration of the Shepherds" in the Prado; "Israelites Departing from Egypt "; and "Cattle Reposing Beneath Rocks," in the Academy of San Fernando.

Orrente died in 1644 at Toledo. Of his school were Pablo Pontons, Esteban March, and Cristobal Garcia Salmeron.

Esteban March, although a Valencian, is rather of the school of the *Naturalisti*, of Toledo, than of his native city. A man of eccentric habit and hot passion, he is said to have prepared himself for his work by beating a drum or blowing a trumpet, and then slashing the walls of his studio with his sword or cutlass. Having worked himself up to a proper pitch of excitement, he would set to work on a canvas, throw on his colour, and dash off a free and vigorous battle-piece. There are an "Encampment of Turks," and a " Passing the Red Sea," in the Prado, each a very bold and spirited specimen of March's realistic style; besides figures of drunkards.

His best pupils were his son Miguel, Senen Vila, and Juan Conchillos Falco.

His most important religious paintings were a "Last Supper," for San Juan del Mercado, at Valencia, and two scenes from the life of St. Francis de Paula for the Minorite Convent.

Jacinto Geronimo de Espinosa was born at Concentayna in 1608. He studied first with his father Geronimo Rodriguez, a second-rate artist of the naturalistic school ; and entered later the studio of Francisco Ribalta. He shows plainly the Italian tradition of that master, in his graceful design, correct composition, and knowledge of chiaro-scuro ; but his strong naturalistic tendency is carried sometimes to excess, as in the " Mocking of Christ by the Jews," in the Prado. Cean Bermudez mentions as among his finest works a " Magdalen," in the Museum at Valencia, and a " Transfiguration," painted for the Carmelite Church ; he thinks that these equal the best works ·of the Bolognese school, and even surpass them in the power of chiaroscuro.

Among Espinosa's chief works were a series of eight large pictures painted in 1638, for the *Carmelitas ;* and in 1655, a series of scenes from the life of San Luis de Beltran, executed for the Church of San Domingo. The Museum of Valencia contains some of his finest paintings.

Espinosa died at Valencia in 1680. His son Miguel Geronimo, Luis Domingo, and Garcia Ferrer were his scholars and imitators.

Josef de Ribera—lo Spagnoletto—was born in 1588 at San Felipe de Xativa, near Valencia. He studied awhile with Ribalta, going later to Italy. Our first account of him there is, that while ragged, half-starved, and destitute he copied the frescoes on the façades of the palaces, or at the shrines on the street corners, a certain wealthy

ST. JEROME.   RIBERA.   MUSEO DEL PRADO.

cardinal saw him, and struck by his evident talent, took him to his palace and provided for all his wants. But Ribera missed his vagabond way of living and the incentive to work given by his poverty. He returned to his street-studies and was soon distinguished among the young painters who followed the style of Caravaggio. His short stature won him the name of Spagnoletto, by which he is known throughout Italy. While adopting Caravaggio's bold manner, he made careful study of Raffaelle and the Carracci ; his subsequent acquaintance with Correggio's works at Parma and Modena is plainly visible in his earlier pictures.

Finding no opening for his talents at Rome, he retired to Naples. There he attached himself to Michael Angelo Caravaggio, whose manner he continued to study. Chancing to attract the interest of a rich picture-dealer, he found a ready market for his sketches, and better still, a rich wife in the dealer's fair daughter. Soon after that his " Martyrdom of St. Bartholomew " pleased the Viceroy, the Duke of Osuña, who bought the picture, while he made Ribera court-painter, with a monthly salary of sixty doubloons, and charge over all the decoration of the palace.

Ribera was now at the head of his profession in Naples ; and surrounded by sycophants and imitators. He gathered about him a band of unprincipled painters who sought, by fair means or foul, to control the public favour. They entered into a regular conspiracy to gain the privi-

lege of painting the Chapel of San Gennaro. Il Cavaliere
d' Arpino, Guido, Gessi, were in turn driven away from
the city and their allotted work. Domenichino fared little
better. His private character was infamously slandered,
his work scoffed at, his life threatened in anonymous
letters; the plasterers were bribed to mix ashes with the
mortar on which his frescoes were to be painted. At last
rendered desperate, Domenichino fled to Rome. In an
evil hour he was persuaded to return; and soon after
died, it is supposed by poison, in 1641. Ribera painted
one altar-piece for the chapel; it represents San Gennaro
led to the furnace whence he escaped unharmed.

Ribera's Italian pictures are too well known to need
mention here; his masterpiece is the *Pietà* in the Church
of San Martino at Naples. He was patronized by the
succeeding Spanish viceroys, Osuña, Alba, Monterey,
Oñate; each in his turn held him in high favour. In 1630
he was elected a member of the Roman Academy of St.
Luke. In 1644 the Pope, Innocent X., sent him the cross
of the Order of Christ.

Ribera was a man of varied social talents, a brilliant
talker, a witty and sarcastic humorist. Among numerous
anecdotes is one connected with his studies in alchemy.
Two Spanish officers, while at his house, engaged in a
serious discussion of the subject. Bored beyond all
endurance by their dull talk, Ribera gravely invited them
to come to his house on the morrow, when, he said, he
would show them the philosopher's stone, which chanced

just then to be in his possession. They came the next day and found Ribera in his studio, at work on a half-length picture of St. Jerome. He prayed them to be seated; finished his picture and sent it away by his servant, receiving in return a small roll of gold pieces. Throwing the gold on the table he exclaimed : " Learn of me how to make gold; I do it by painting, you by serving the king. Diligent labour is the true alchemy."

Ribera died at Naples in 1656.

In his earlier works we find traces of the style of Cor-reggio and the great Venetian masters. It is to them that he owes his brilliancy of colour. But his later pictures have the exaggerated and gloomy force of the *Naturalisti.* A chief feature of this school was their love of exaggerated, anatomical drawing. It is the great fault the artist feels in Ribera, whose figures are drawn with such bony and unfleshed vigour as often to startle us into wonder at his power; but often, in these anatomical efforts, all the grace and health of art are lost. We do not want to meet a walking skeleton in life or in art. An artist is not a dissector; and though Ribera is a powerful genius, we look at his pictures with mingled wonder and disgust. He unbares all the hideous secrets of human life. His characters and scenes create our disgust. His amazing subtlety in depicting horrors wearies us. The grace of nature and life is torn off, and only the grim spectre stalks about.

Spain possesses **many of his finest works.** In Vittoria, Granada, Valencia, Cordova, Valladolid, Zaragoza, and Salamanca are important paintings of Ribera; and also in the churches and convents of Madrid. The Prado, alone, has fifty-eight of his pictures. Many of these are figures of the apostles and saints. The finest are St. Andrew, St. Bartholomew, St. Simon, St. Paul the Hermit, and St. Jerome; all these are gaunt, fleshless figures, but very striking in their gloomy vigour. Most powerful and horrible is the "Martyrdom of St. Bartholomew," a favourite subject of his, but few ever wish to see it twice. Ribera has treated his "Jacob's Dream" in a different style; it shows clearly his study of Correggio. The general effect is very striking :—a monk in his brown frock is asleep near the stump of a tree, his head resting on a stone; while in the far distance we see the dim ladder and a few angel forms half hidden by the clouds. In the Cathedral of Valencia is an "Adoration of Shepherds" wherein the Virgin is a marvel of calm beauty.

Among the most remarkable men of the school of Seville was Pablo de Cespedes, born at Cordova in 1538. He passed many years in Italy, where he studied the manner of Michael Angelo, and formed an intimate acquaintance with Federigo Zuccaro, in connection with whom he executed several frescoes in the Trinità del Monte. He painted several pictures for San Carlo in the Corso; and painted, in fresco, in the Aracœli some cherubs over the tomb of the Marquis of Saluzzo. His chief piece of sculpture was a head of Seneca, which he modelled to fit an antique trunk; this work was much admired, and beneath it was found, written by an unknown hand, "*Victor il Spagnuolo.*" Cespedes was known in Italy by the name of Paolo de Cordova or Cedaspe. In 1577, while yet at Rome, he was appointed Canon of the Cathedral of Cordova. There he passed the remainder of his life, making an annual visit to Seville during his vacation. His was a many-sided genius; painter, sculptor, architect, antiquary, poet, and writer of a noble prose. He died at Cordova in 1608 at the age of seventy.

Cespedes published an essay on the Cathedral of Cordova to prove that it stood on the site of an ancient temple of Janus, and another on the temple of Solomon and the origin of the Corinthian architecture; but his chief literary work was entitled, *De la Comparacion de la antigua y moderna Pintura y Escultura*—"A Comparison of Ancient and Modern Painting and Sculpture." It is written in a chaste and noble style, and is a delightful work. In his preface he regrets that he has so little time for his classics. "Still," says the artist-scholar, " I do read somewhat of Pindar, for whom I have ever had a special admiration, and into whom I can never dip so lightly but I find some correct and glowing picture worthy of the great Michael Angelo."[1] He brings before us a rich and living study of ancient literature and art, of history and biography; not the rules of art, but the living fruit and flowers.

---

[1] Stirling-Maxwell, p. 327.

His graphic description of all he has seen in his travels
has a marvellous charm, and shows a keen insight into all
the problems of social life. His clear and intelligent
comparison of antique and modern art shows rare critical
power. Cespedes also wrote a treatise on Perspective
which has unfortunately perished. It is to his pen that
we owe the noblest didactic poem on art in the Spanish, or, indeed, in any language. We have some frag-
ments of it embalmed in Pacheco. Poetry with him is
not the jingling of metre or the elaborate fretwork of art,
or the toy of literary idleness. It is the noblest product
of his mind and heart. With him poetry is not fable; it
is the ideal side of reality. He knows that there is much
and more of poetic material in his age of science than in
the earliest time ; and as we open his first book, we feel
that we are reading a grand poem, the rocks speak, and
nature sings to us of the divine origin of art and the
power of the "Painter of the world." As he describes the
implements of the writer's art he recalls the immortal
past ; he feels that the poet is the prophet of his time ;
its voice uttering the spirit of the people ; and that in
Homer we read the living mind of Greece—his verse is
history. It is he, not the Stygian flood, which has made
an Achilles immortal. The mighty cities, Troy, Athens,
Rome, lie in ruins ; and yet to us their human life is as
full of heights and depths, of mysteries of faith, and love,
and courage, and suffering, as in the day of Homer. His
second book touches on design; in it he describes with

marvellous power and life the war-horse—the noble Spanish steed. Perspective, foreshortening, and copying are
next treated. Here the fragment ends.

But we must come back to the painter. Pacheco says
that " he was a great imitator of Correggio and one of the
best colorists in Spain. It was to him that the Andalusian school owed the fine tone of their flesh-tints." In
proof of this he mentions Cespedes' *retablo* in the Jesuit
College, and his many works in Cordova and Seville.
" Had Cespedes," says Ponz, "been the friend and follower of Raffaelle, as he was of Zuccaro, he had been one
of the greatest as well as the most learned of painters."
Cean Bermudez praises his grandeur and elegance of
design, his powerful figures, showing a careful study of
anatomy, his skill in foreshortening, his effects of light
and shade, his brilliant colour, his true expression, and,
above all, his invention, which gave him no need to beg
from others.

His finest works were executed for the Jesuit College
of St. Catharine at Cordova, and represented scenes
from the life of this saint, and other sacred subjects.
No trace is left of these pictures. In the cathedral at
Cordova is his "Last Supper," a work that is worthy
to be placed by that of Juanes. Cean Bermudez says
that "it is above all remarkable for its fine arrangement
of the subject, the expression of the heads, the holy
affection of the apostles, the angelic beauty of the
Christ, the sordid treachery of Judas. It is of this that

the well-known story is told that the artist, in painting the "Last Supper," put into the foreground an exquisite vase. When his friends came to see his work, each said: "What lovely chasing on this vase!" "Andres," cried the artist, "paint out this vase, remove it entirely, since no one sees the many persons, the many faces and attitudes I have drawn with such careful study." Cespedes could bear criticism with but little patience; one day a friend, whose portrait he was sketching in black chalk, said that he could not see any likeness in the sketch. "Do you not know," exclaimed Cespedes, hastily, "that it matters little nowadays whether a portrait is like or not; it is quite enough, my dear sir, if it prove an effective head." Many of Cespedes' finest works have perished; but in the *Contaduna Mayor* at Seville, there yet remain a representation of the "Sacrifice of Abraham," and Sta. Justa and Sta. Rufina bearing their tower between them.

Of the school of Cespedes were Juan Luis Zambrano, Antonio Mohedano, Juan de Peñalosa, Antonio de Contreras, and Christobal Vela.

Pedro de Villegas Marmolejo was born at Seville in 1520. He studied in Italy, and followed closely in the manner of Raffaelle and of the noblest traditions of the Roman school.

In the Cathedral at Seville is his fine picture of the "Visitation." It is a simple, grand composition, with pure design and admirable colour, and recalls strongly the

manner of Pedro Campaña. On the side panels are represented "San Blas" and the "Baptism of Christ," "San
Sebastian," and "San Roque." Above them hangs an
exquisite infant Christ surrounded by cherubs. In the
Hospital of San Lazaro, without the city walls, is a noble
picture of that saint in full pontifical robes, and in the
Church of San Lorenzo, an " Annunciation " and a. " Virgin and Child," beneath which the painter was buried in
1597.

In Francisco Pacheco it is not the painter whom we
most respect, but the careful writer and the learned
author of the *Arte de la Pintura.* His treatise is a
classic, an excellent formula of didactic rules, but in the
philosophic portion he loses all value; he is a casuist,
a definer of each detail in attitude or costume, a rigorous
formalist. A narrow mysticism with him took too much
the place of his own thought, and of the real sources
of knowledge. Books, like other arts of civilization, have
this for their value, that they help us like a microscope to
see more than with our naked eyes—but too often they
injure the sight. Pacheco put on the near-sighted glasses
of the Inquisition and looked only through their myopic
lenses. But the historical portion of his work is valuable
so far as it relates to his own age and country. He is
long in coming to his proper subject; he discourses of art
from the creation to his own time, and he wearies us with
anecdotes of Athenian and Rhodian painters. But when
he reaches his own age his record has real worth and

interest. His history is the storehouse whence all later writers have drawn their knowledge. He shows a cordial admiration of his fellow artists, and a strong affection for his pupil and son-in-law Velazquez, which win our hearty sympathy.

Pacheco was born at Seville in 1571. He studied under Luis Fernandez, and shows plainly the worst traditions of the Roman school,—a dry, harsh colour, and a lack of force and breadth of treatment. In 1611 he visited Toledo and Madrid where he met El Greco, Vicente Carducho, and other distinguished painters; and on his return to Seville he opened a school of painting. In the following year he executed his most important work, the "Last Judgment," for the Convent of Santa Isabel. He was a careful and constant painter, and his works are spread throughout Andalusia. His house was a meeting-place for the artists and literary men of his day. Pacheco himself was no mean poet: it is on his pen rather than on his pencil that his fame rests. Five years after the appearance of his *Arte de la Pintura*, he died at Seville (1654).

FORGE OF VULCAN.   VELAZQUEZ.   MUSEO DEL PRADO.

VI.

SEVILLE.

WE are apt to read the history of art in a fragmentary way; and so reading it, to regard the great Spanish painters as if they were a few isolated men, who stood apart from their race. But we must look on that age, as upon other creative ages, as the awakening not here and there of an individual, but of the mind of a whole people; and also as the particular education of the artist mind until it passes beyond its earlier, partial utterances to the majesty of a Zurbaran, and at last rises into the burning light of a Velazquez, the heavenly vision of a Murillo. In a word this history is the preparation for a grand national art. We do not mean by this to trace in every obscure Spanish painter a type of the great age of art, but mean that we find in the germ the preparation for the flowers.

It is the living picture of the whole time which we see pass before us; a book in which we read the mind and heart of a nation. What art of any time combines in it more varied elements of strength! Here are the homely pictures drawn from common life, and yet the splendour of poetic thought, the tender grace of Cano, the vigour of Ribera, the spiritual conceptions of Murillo, the grandeur of Zurbaran. It is a gradual revelation; like a whisper in the earlier artists, it grows a broader and fuller voice in the later, until it bursts in the mighty accents of Velazquez.

In the great epochs of life, whether in religion or art or letters, we find this universal law, that the man who leads the age is he who has winnowed the dusty chamber of opinions with a knowledge drawn from living sources. Luther goes back from the scholastic divinity to the personal faith in the Christian soul. Descartes studies his own mind, and the insight of his volume outreaches all the earlier speculative theories. Cowper restores English taste, bringing it back from artificial standards to the simple life of the English hearth and home. Velazquez rises from Pacheco's teaching to the truer, simpler master—Nature. It is the sure sign of decay when the main purpose of art or literature is to defend the old system, when age on age must repeat the definitions of Fernandez or the style of Luis de Vargas. Education means above all the leading forth of the mental powers of the man. Art tradition cannot take the place of our own minds, and of the real sources of knowledge, which are always fresh, and as living as in the past. The study of anatomy is useless without acquaintance with the living man. The knowledge of perspective cannot serve instead of nature itself. Each artist has before him the same fresh world of God, and all our treatises on painting are only an imperfect commentary on the book written in each mind. All history only opens to us a chapter of the same human nature and human life that we see to-day in the social world. And here is always the essential difference between the thinker and the pedant, that the one studies the original, and the other studies the poor copy. Hence it is you find in a Roelas a knowledge of human life which surpasses the theories of Pacheco.

Roelas is the first of the great Sevillian school. Essentially Venetian in colour, he unites with fair colour a grand design, and strong, broad handling ; he is the first and one of the noblest of the realistic school.

The licentiate Juan de las Roelas was born at Seville in 1558 or 1560. He studied for some time in Italy, probably at Venice. In 1603 he was appointed to a prebend in the Collegiate Church of Olivarez, for which his earliest works—four scenes from the life of the Virgin—were executed. He relinquished his stall a few years later, passing his time either at Seville or Madrid. In 1624 he was appointed canon at Olivarez, where he died in 1625.

In the Cathedral at Seville is a fine picture of "Santiago Destroying the Moors at the Battle of Clavijo," a grand, vigorous composition, executed in 1609. "The horse is not equal to the rest, but the saint is bursting on the infidel foe with the terrors of the whirlwind."[1] Cean Bermudez praises " its force, grandeur, and Titianesque touches." The " Martyrdom of St. Andrew," now in the Museum at

---

[1] Head, p. 106.

Seville was executed for the Colegio di Santo Tomas. It recalls Tintoretto in colour and general treatment, though the tone is redder and the landscape has grown rather too blue. This work was executed for the Flemish chapel at Santo Tomas; as it was not ready at the time agreed on, and was finished hastily, the college authorities refused to pay the stipulated amount of one thousand ducats. Roelas, on the other hand, now demanded two thousand. The picture was accordingly sent to Flanders for valuation, whence it returned with an award of triple the original sum, which was paid to Roelas.

In the University, once the Jesuit College, are three fine works of Roelas. A "Holy Family," with St. Ignatius and St. Ignatius Loyola; a "Nativity," and an "Adoration of Shepherds." But his noblest work is the "Death of St. Isidore," in the church of that saint. The composition is simple and grand. In the foreground kneels the dying saint, supported by his sorrowing clergy; near them are some beautiful choir-boys, while in the background are gathered the grief-stricken people. Above are the Saviour and the Virgin holding triumphal crowns; beneath them hover a charming group of angels and cherubs. "For majesty of design, depth of feeling, richness of colour, and for the various beauty of the heads, and the perfect mastery which the painter has displayed in the use of his materials, this altar-piece may be ranked amongst the greatest productions of the pencil. The noble subject has been treated in a style worthy of itself; and the work,

in the opinion of an able English critic, need not shrink
from comparison with the 'great picture on a similar subject—Domenichino's "St. Jerome."' "' There is but one
work of Roelas in the Prado. It was formerly in the palace of Aranjuez, and represents "Moses Striking the
Rock."

Roelas had but few scholars; chief of these were Francisco Varela, a faithful follower of his master's manner;
and Francisco Zurbaran.

One of the most important names of this great age is
that of Francisco de Herrera (*el Viejo*), a worthy pre-
cursor of Zurbaran and Velazquez. Rough and violent
in temper, his style is an outgrowth of the man himself.
Born at Seville about 1576, he early studied in the school
of Luis Fernandez, but soon left that master to devote
himself to the Venetian colour and broad handling of
Roelas.

Herrera's earliest composition, a "Last Judgment," in
the Church of San Bernardo, is a powerful and original
work. In the upper part of the picture appears the Lord as
Judge, attended by the apostles and angels; below stands
St. Michael, with a drawn sword of flame, between the
righteous and the condemned, whose grouping is admirable. It is a magnificent composition; noble in colour,
displaying thorough knowledge of anatomy and ability to
handle the nude; and it is treated in a broad, vigorous
manner. Herrera painted much in fresco—a process well

---

[1] Stirling-Maxwell, pp. 451, 452.

fitted to his bold, dashing style ; but his frescoes have all perished.

El Viejo soon gathered about him a group of distinguished pupils: his two sons—Herrera *el Rubio*, an artist of great prominence who died young; Herrera *el Mozo*,—Diego Velazquez, Francisco de Reina, Sebastian de Llaños, Iriarte, and others of less note. His influence on their style was most powerful, but his coarse and brutal treatment drove them from his studio. They bore away, however, the stamp of his teaching. There is a tradition that when thus left alone, with no one to prepare his palettes or assist him in any way, he was wont to employ his maid-servant to cover his canvas with paint, smeared on with a coarse brush, when he worked the rough masses of wet colour into drapery and figure.

Herrera engraved much on copper, and was accused of coining. He took refuge in the Jesuit College of St. Hermenegild, and while there painted for the high altar "the Triumph of St. Hermenegild." It is now in the Museum, and has been much repainted. It possesses a brilliancy of colour, a grandeur of design, a bold, free handling, and rich tone never surpassed by the master. It was to this picture that he owed his freedom ; for the king, on seeing it, sent for him and said : "What need of other wealth has a man who owns such skill, go—you are free; but beware lest this mishap again befall you."

More brutal and harsh than before, Herrera returned

to his home; his daughter, unable to bear with him any longer, sought refuge in a convent; his younger son robbed him and fled to Rome; the elder, *el Rubio*, was long since dead. Hardened by misfortune, broken with grief and years, Herrera forgot all in work. For the Archbishop's palace he painted "The Israelites Gathering Manna," "Moses Smiting the Rock," "The Marriage of Cana," and the "Miracles of Loaves and Fishes," and for numerous churches and convents he executed works in fresco. In 1650 he went to Madrid. To this period belong two pictures painted for the *Cartuxa* at Paular, and a scene from the life of San Ramon for the *Mercenarios Calzadas*. He died in 1656.

Francisco Herrera, *el Mozo* (the younger), born at Seville in 1622, inherited his father's irascible disposition, his very worst characteristics without his genius. A skilful painter, a fine colourist, he is wanting in force and originality, in the bold, dashing vigour of *el Viejo*. Palomino tells us that he was always jealous of his fellow painters, and suspected them of the same feeling. He inscribed his name on a stucco-scroll, gnawed by lizards, on the dome of our Lady of Atocha; in a picture of San Vicente Ferrer he painted a dog mouthing the jaw-bone of an ass; and elsewhere he symbolized the supposed jealousy of his rivals by writing his name on a piece of paper that the rats tore into shreds. He was very careful of his dignity and avenged any supposed slight by a scathing caricature. A grandee having employed him to choose some paintings for his gallery at a certain sale of pictures, went later in person to the sale, and preferred several poor works to the admirable selections of the painter. Highly incensed, Herrera drew a monkey, who, grinning with delight, plucked a thistle from a bed of roses. He was with difficulty dissuaded from sending the clever sketch to the nobleman whom he thus ridiculed.

Herrera studied awhile at Rome, gaining the name of *Lo Spagnuolo dei Pesci*, from his skill in executing fish in subjects of still life, or *bodegones*. In 1656, after his father's death, he returned to Seville. His first picture was executed for the chapel of the "Holy Sacrament" in the *Sagrario* of the cathedral. It represented the doctors of the church adoring the Host and the Immaculate Conception. It is one of his best works, though lacking force ; and, like all his compositions, mannered and affected. "The same qualities of softness and affectation characterize the angel in the picture of St. Francis in the cathedral; the saint himself is fine, and altogether this last is one of the painter's best works.[1] In 1660, when the Academy of Art was founded, Herrera was chosen vice-president ; but whether from jealousy of Murillo, the president, or for some other cause, he soon resigned and went to Madrid. Soon after his arrival there he painted for the *Carmelitas Descalzos* an altar-piece, now in the Prado, representing the Triumph of St. Hermenegild. He also decorated in fresco the choir of "San Felipe el Real,"

---

[1] Head, p. 115.

and the dome of Our Lady of Atocha. Herrera was made painter to the king, and in 1671, master of the royal works in the room of Gaspar de Peña. He died at Madrid in 1685.

Agustin del Castillo was born at Seville in 1565. He was a pupil of Luis Fernandez, and followed closely in the tradition of the Italian school. A skilful fresco painter, he has left traces of his work throughout Cordova. Unhappily, the greater portion of his frescoes were executed for positions out-of-doors, and have thus perished, or, at least, have been barbarously restored. In the cathedral is a "Conception of the Virgin," which shows a correct modelling and a noble, pure design, but is sadly wanting in colour. In his "Adoration of Kings," in the cathedral at Cadiz, there is a marked change of style: it shows clearly the influence of the Naturalistic school.

Agustin del Castillo died at Cordova in 1626.

Juan del Castillo was born at Seville in 1584. Like his elder brother, he, too, studied under Luis Fernandez ; but he early cast off the Italian fetters and followed the *Naturalisti* of his time. The brilliant character of Roelas had a marked influence on the young painter. He was the contemporary of Herrera, and the first to teach *naturalism* in a regular manner. His fame rests rather on his pupils than on his own pictures, which were hard and dry. They are often mistaken for those of the Italian period, or are attributed to one of his pupils. In the Church of *Regina Angelorum* is a "Virgin of the Rosary," attended by St. Peter and St. Paul, which is called the early work of Murillo; and in the Church of Monte Sion is a *retablo*, on the centre panel of which is represented the "Assumption of the Virgin," and the "Coronation"; on the side panels are the "Annunciation," the "Nativity of the Virgin," the "Visitation," and "Adoration of Kings"; at the base are the doctors of the church with Bonaventura and Thomas Aquinas. In the Museum of Seville are five pictures taken from the suppressed convents. These paintings are in the best manner of Castillo, and are a fair example of the period of transition from the Italian tradition to the free Spanish *Naturalism*.

Juan del Castillo died at Cadiz in 1640. The most noted of his scholars were Murillo, Alonso Cano, Pedro de Moya, Pedro de Medina Valbuena, and Andres de Medina.

Antonio del Castillo y Saavedra, the son of Agustin, studied with his father. At the death of the latter, in 1625, he entered the studio of Francisco Zurbaran. He seems to have gained nothing from Zurbaran's teaching but an exaggerated violence and harshness. He often has a powerful design, but no command of colour. Palomino relates that Cano, on looking at some of Castillo's pictures, exclaimed: "It is a pity that Antonio does not come to Granada and learn colour; he draws so well." On hearing this remark, Castillo retorted: "It were better that Alonso Cano came here; we would repay his good in-

tentions by teaching him to draw." Castillo was a man
of letters, a pleasant versifier, and full of humour, though
somewhat spoiled by the adulation offered him in his native city. When his former pupil, Juan de Alfaro, came
to Cordova, young, arrogant, fresh from the school of
Velazquez, he adopted a conceited habit of signing his pictures most conspicuously "*Alfaro pinxit*." Castillo re-
buked his vanity by inscribing a "Baptism of Christ," in
the Capuchin Convent, where, too, were sundry works of
the younger artist, "*non pinxit Alfaro*."

Antonio Castillo early established himself at Cordova,
where he painted a *retablo* for the Chapel of San Acisclo,
and a "Virgin del Rosario," "St. Roque," "St. Sebastian," and a large picture of "St. Pelagius Hearing his
Death Sentence." He also decorated the stairway of the
Convent of San Pablo; this painting represented St.
Ferdinand consecrating to St. Paul the convent he has
builded. For the Hospital of Jesus Nazareno he executed, in oil, a picture of the "Making of the Cross,"
and the "Penitent Thief," and for the *Franciscanos* he
was employed in several important works. In the Prado
is only one specimen of his painting—an "Adoration of
Shepherds."

Antonio del Castillo died at Cordova in 1667. His
chief pupils were Valdes Leal, Juan de Alfaro, and Pedro
Antonio.

We come now to a painter who stands foremost in the
annals of Spanish art; although we cannot, as did

Philip IV., call Zurbaran "*Pintor del Rey y Rey de los pintores.*" We recognize in him not the highest gift of original power of inspiration; yet we must award him his just honour as among the strongest pillars of Spanish art.

Francisco Zurbaran was born of humble parents at Fuente de Cantos, in Estramadura in 1598; without education or rank he had yet in him the elements of a great painter. At an early age he went to Seville where he studied under Roelas; but then, as ever, nature was his best master. His drapery was always painted from the lay figure, and his flesh-tints from nature.

Zurbaran was not an elaborate painter like Velazquez; he painted heads admirably, but he had none of Velazquez' marvellous skill in photographing a group of figures at varied distances; he lacks, too, his sparkle and airy grace. Nor is he a mild, suave spirit like Murillo: we miss the soft and rounded outlines and harmonious colour of that master. His is a bold, robust, energetic nature, a grander far than Caravaggio, but with much of that artist's power; we find in him great breadth of handling, careful study of drapery, and love of strong contrast, with the sombre tone so characteristic of Spanish art; but with a depth and brilliancy of tone that recalls Rembrandt. He was the great painter of the Spanish Carthusian, as Roelas was the painter of the Jesuit, and Murillo of the Franciscan. It is to this choice of subjects that he doubtless owes his noble treatment of drapery. Schepeler says

"that it is most important to distinguish the *cast* of
drapery from the *execution* of it. Though no painter ever
executed white linen better than Murillo, yet we miss in
most Spanish pictures that simple dignity which is the
charm of the drapery of the early Italian masters. The
architectural principle of stiffness which prevails throughout the old Italian pictures, gave to the drapery of the
early masters a broad and noble dignity. This is not
wholly lacking in Spanish art. The dress of the religious
orders gave fine models for such excellence. The masterpiece of Zurbaran, in the College of Santo Tomas, lacks
neither dignity nor breadth in the drapery; but the cast
of drapery in many pictures where the religious orders are
not represented, is unsatisfactory. There was no new
principle in Spain, as there was in Italy, ready to take the
place of the stiff symmetry of the early masters. The
study of the antique in the fifteenth century, joined to
their direct study of nature, gave a new source of beauty
and dignity. There was little opportunity for Spanish
artists to study the antique, and the Holy Office hindered
all study from nature. In a country where there were
such rules as, that the Virgin might not be represented
with uncovered feet, no drapery could be what Goethe calls
' the thousand-fold echo of the form,' even had such excellence been desired."

In 1625 Zurbaran painted for the cathedral at Seville
a series of scenes from the life of St. Peter; and in the
same year he executed his master-work for the Colegio

di San Tomas Aquino. " The Virgin and Christ are above
in glory with St. Paul and St. Dominic, whilst below is
St. Thomas Aquinas with the four Doctors of the Latin
Church; nearest of all kneel the Emperor Charles V., in
his imperial crown and mantle, and the Archbishop Diego
Deza, who was the founder of the college. The two
latter figures are inimitable, nor is the figure of St. Jerome, with his uplifted finger, and the expression of deep
thought on his face, at all less striking; a broad mass of
shadow is thrown across the lower part, but the background
is sunny; the composition is simple and the style severe
and massive. The head of St. Thomas was a portrait of
Don Agostin de Escobar." [1]

In his picture of San Pedro de Alcantara, there is what
enfolds most powerfully the secret of painting, its ability
to body forth the spiritual. It is the eye of the saint in his
rapt utterance, and it conveys indeed that conception in
its fulness; not the eye of the common observer, gazing
on visible things before him; not the eye of the philosopher, seeing vague forms in its blank abstraction, but the
keen eye of the imagination, shaping the unseen thought
in all the distinctness of reality. " Seeing the invisible,"
in the language of St. Paul.

Zurbaran's works were scattered throughout his native
Andalusia; each convent shared in his talent. For the
Merced Calzada and the *Mercenarios Descalzos* he painted
a number of passages in the life of San Pedro Nolasco.

---

[1] Head, pp. 128, 129.

For the *Cartuxa* of Xeres he executed a series from the life of our Lord, and of the Evangelists, and other saints. The *Trinitarios* and the *Capuchinos* boasted his noble paintings; for the *Cartuxa* of Santa Maria de los Cuevas he finished three pictures representing St. Bruno conversing with Pope Urban II.; St. Hugo visiting a refectory, where the monks were unlawfully dining upon flesh-meat; and the Virgin spreading her mantle over a group of Carthusian monks. "The second is the best of the three, and is curious as a scene of the old monastic life of Spain, whence the cowled friar has passed away like the mailed knight. At a table, spread with what seems a very frugal meal, sit seven Carthusians in white, some of them with their high peaked hoods drawn over their heads; the aged bishop Hugo in purple vestments, and attended by a page, stands in the foreground; over the heads of the monks there hangs a picture of the Virgin; and an open door affords a glimpse of a distant church. These venerable friars seem portraits; each differs in feature from the other, yet all bear the impress of long years of solitary and silent penance; their white draperies chill the eye, as their cold hopeless faces chill the heart; and the whole scene is brought before us with a vivid fidelity, which shows that Zurbaran studied the Carthusian in his native cloisters, with the like close and fruitful attention that Velazquez bestowed on the courtier, strutting it in the corridors of the Alcazar or the alleys of Aranjuez." [1]

---

[1] Stirling-Maxwell, pp. 771, 772.

These pictures are now in the *Museo del Merced*, which contains several other important works of Zurbaran: among which are a delightful Infant Christ wearing a crown of thorns, and the admirable figures of three bishops.

Zurbaran was called to Madrid in 1650 through Velazquez's influence. He was then made painter to the king; he decorated several of the royal palaces; painting at the Buenretiro the "Labours of Hercules," a series of ten pictures, now in the Prado. Besides these there are two scenes from the life of San Pedro Nolasco, formerly in the *Merced Calzada* at Seville; and an exquisite picture of the Infant Christ lying asleep on a cross, wrapt in royal purple.

Zurbaran died at Madrid in 1662. Of his school were Bernabe de Ayala, the brothers Polancos, and several other admirable Sevillian painters.

In strong contrast with Zurbaran appear the life and works of Alonso Cano. A man of violent passions, jealous and irritable in disposition, and most eccentric in character, you find in his paintings a simple, pure design; a calm, tender sentiment; a harmony of nature and art, and a tone of refined beauty that brings repose after a busy journey through the sombre corridor of Spanish *naturalism*.

Born at Granada in 1601, the son of a designer and carver of *retablos*, Cano studied his art at Seville under Castillo and Pacheco; he also entered the studio of the famous sculptor Montañes. He learned, however, much more from certain antique statues in the *Casa de Pilatus* in the palace of the Duke of Alcala than from any in-struction of Montañes, who was a follower of the exag-gerated school of Michael Angelo. Some of Cano's coloured sculpture is marvellously beautiful.

Cano's genius soon placed him in the foremost rank of Sevillian artists; but in 1637, a duel with Sebastiano de Llaños y Valdes, in which the latter was severely wounded, forced him to fly to Madrid. There, his friend and fellow-pupil of Pacheco, Velazquez, presented him to the Conde-duque de Olivarez. Cano was appointed painter to the king, and drawing-master to Don Baltasar Carlos. He was also chosen to superintend certain works in the royal palaces. To this period belong the many paintings and statues which are met with in the churches and convents of Madrid; in San Isidro el real, Santiago, San Gines, Santa Maria, and the Carmelite and Benedic-tine convents.

In 1644 Cano's wife was murdered; suspicion fell on the artist himself, who fled to Valencia, and took refuge in the Convent of Portacœli, for which he executed seven large pictures. On his return to Madrid he was seized and put to the question with extreme rigour, al-though by the king's orders his right hand was spared. Passing unflinched through the severe ordeal, the artist was declared innocent.

Cano remained at Madrid until 1650, when he was

called to Toledo to give his advice touching certain works
in the cathedral.   In the following year he was appointed
a *racionero* or minor canon in the Cathedral of Granada, on
condition of taking orders during the year.   Not having ful-
filled this condition he lost the stall.   He was appointed
soon after to a chaplaincy to the Bishop of Salamanca,
and with it he was restored to his prebend at Granada.
Cano died in 1667.

In the little incidents repeated by Palomino we catch,
as in a bold etching, the portrait of the whole man, as
well as in a finished picture.   No poor man ever asked
an alms from him in vain, yet he could not bear the sight
or touch of a wretched Jew; impetuous and irritable, he
passed the last years of his life in pious acts and in charity.
His life is a story of singular inconsistency.   Certain anecdotes which Palomino gives us are so characteristic of
the man and the age that they are well worth quoting
here.

When Cano was appointed canon of the Cathedral of
Granada, certain of the chapter appealed to the king on
the ground that the painter lacked sufficient learning.
" It is well," said the king ; " for were Alonso Cano a man
of letters, who knows but we should have made him Archbishop of Toledo.   Go,—men like you we can make, God
alone can create a man like Alonso Cano."

Cano's favourite work was sculpture.   When wearied
with painting he would lay aside his brush and calling for
a chisel block out a statue, and so rest himself.   A pupil

one day remarked that to lay down a brush and take up a
mallet was a strange mode of repose. "Blockhead,"
exclaimed Cano, "do you not know that to create form
and relief on a flat surface, is a greater labour than to
fashion one shape into another?"

An auditor (*oidor*) of the Chancery ordered of Cano a
statue, about a yard in height, of St. Anthony of Padua,
to whom he bore especial devotion. When the work
was completed he came to see it, was well pleased, and in-
quired its cost. Cano replied, "one hundred doubloons."
After an astonished pause his patron asked how many
days he had spent on it. "Twenty-five," answered the
artist. "Then," said the patron, "you reckon your work
at four doubloons a day?" "Your lordship reckons
wrong," replied Cano, "for I have spent fifty years learning to make this statue in twenty-five days." "And I"
retorted the auditor, "have spent my youth and my
patrimony in studying at the university, and now auditor
of Granada, a far nobler profession than yours—I get but
a doubloon a day." Cano remembered the king's
words, and crying "a nobler profession indeed! the
king can make auditors of the dust of the earth, but it is
reserved to God alone to make an Alonso Cano," he
dashed the figure of St. Anthony on the floor. The
auditor fled in haste, not knowing what Cano might do
next. "To offend such a man" says Palomino, "as an
auditor of Granada, who is a little god upon earth, was
not wise"; and it resulted in the canon's stall being

declared vacant because he had not taken orders within the given time.

No mediæval saint held a Jew in greater horror than Cano. When in his walks through the narrow streets of Granada, he met a wretched Israelite, in his *sanbenito*, the yellow gown imposed by the Inquisition, he crossed the street, or stood within a door-way, for fear that the unbeliever should brush against him. Whenever that happened, he cast aside the unclean garment and sent to his house for another. Sometimes, when not sure that the Jew had touched him, he would ask his servant, who always assured him that it was a mere touch of no importance, well aware that the infected garment would then be thrown to him. He could not, however, wear the unclean clothing on pain of dismissal. One day Cano discovered his house-keeper, a new-comer who did not know his peculiar prejudice, bargaining with a Jewish hawker. Greatly enraged he hurried in search of a stick or a poker; while the terrified Jew fled away, and the house-keeper, afraid of a beating, hid herself in a neighbor's house. She was only received back after a proper quarantine and strict inquiry as to whether she had Jewish kin or acquaintance. The spot on which the unhappy Jew had stood was repaved and the canon's shoes given to his servant. In 1667 Cano was very poor and ill: we learn from two entries in the records of the Chapter that a grant of five hundred reals was made to Alonso Cano, " being sick and very poor, and unable to pay the doctor "; the second entry states that two hundred reals were given him to buy poultry and sweetmeats. His illness proving mortal, the priest of the parish, which was Santiago in the Albaycin, the quarter in which was the prison of the Inquisition, came to see him and desired to administer the sacrament after confession. Cano asked him if he administered it to Jews condemned by the Holy Office. The priest answered that he did so. "Then" cried Cano, "Senor Licenciado, go with God (*se vaya con Dios*), and do not trouble yourself to call again; for he who communicates with the penitent Jews shall never communicate with me." The curate of San Andres was then sent for. On his arrival he put into the artist's hand a rudely carved crucifix, which Cano thrust aside. "My son," said the priest, "what dost thou do? This is the Lord who redeemed thee and who alone can save thee." "I believe it, father," replied the dying man; "yet vex me not with this wretched thing to deliver me over to the devil,—give me a simple cross, that with it I may reverence Christ in faith; I can worship him as he is in himself, and as I contemplate him in my own mind." "This being done, he died" says Palomino, "in a most exemplary manner, edifying all those about him."

Cano never hesitated to adopt the ideas of others in his painting. He borrowed much from prints, employing a hint given even by the coarse wood-cuts on top of a ballad. He acknowledged and excused such usage. "Do the same thing with the same effect," he would say to those who objected to this practice, "and I will forgive you." He had not Zurbaran's ready brush. Although an able draughtsman, yet, busied with the other branches of his art, he has left few large pictures behind him.

Cano was a lover of the antique, and we see his careful study in his mastery of the nude subjects which were commonly avoided by Spanish painters, and also in his chaste design and fine drapery. His colour is rich, though somewhat cold, and his sentiment pure and tender; the beauty of his noble style is that in which an harmonious effect is produced by the blending of fair colour and classic severity of form. We have not here the powerful mass or outline of some masters of style, but the depth and completeness of a finished picture.

In the parish church of Getafé, a village two leagues from Madrid, is a *retablo* with six scenes from the life of Mary Magdalene. The best are the second and the fourth ;. the former represents the Magdalene washing the Lord's feet in the house of Simon. It is executed in Cano's best manner. There are much power and varied expression in the figures of the Pharisee and his guests. In the fourth the Magdalene is kneeling at the feet of Christ, who wears a broad palmer's hat. Over two of the side altars are other works of Cano. Several of these represent figures of saints. The finest is an " Ecce Homo."

In the cathedral at Granada are some of Cano's noblest works. Seven of these are grand pictures representing passages in the life of the Virgin. In the *Capilla di San Miguel* is a " Virgin de la Soledad." In the *Capilla del Carmen* are two fine heads of St. Paul and St. John Baptist. In the *Trinidad* are several pictures. In the *Capilla Real* is a " Descent from the Cross," one of Cano's best works. In the cathedral at Malaga is a fine example of this painter—a " Virgin del Rosario," enthroned on clouds and adored by a group of six saintly figures. The *Museo del Merced* contains one specimen of Cano ; but elsewhere in Seville are numerous and important works. In the University is a St. John Evangelist and a St. John Baptist. In the Chapel of *Las Reliquias* are several pictures representing St. Cosmo and St. Damian, a " Saviour," and a " Holy Father." In San Vicente is a " Descent from the Cross." " The most beautiful and one of the latest of Cano's pictures is that of Our Lady of Belem, or Bethlehem, painted at Malaga, for Don Andres Cascantes, who gave it to the Cathedral of Seville, of which he was a minor canon. There it still hangs to the left of the door leading to the court of orange-trees, in a small dark chapel, where it can be seen only by the light of votive tapers. In serene celestial beauty this Madonna is excelled by no image of the blessed Mary ever devised in Spain. Her glorious countenance lends credit to the legends of elder art, and might have visited the slumbers of Becerra, or been revealed in answer to the prayers of Vargas or of Joanes. She more nearly resembles the carved Virgin at Lebrija than any other of Cano's works, and the draperies are in both cases the same colour—a crimson robe, with a dark blue mantle drawn over the head. The head of the divine babe is, perhaps, not sufficiently childlike; but there is much infantine simplicity and grace in his attitude, as he sits with his tiny hand resting on that of his mother. These hands are, as usual, admirably painted; and the whole picture is finished with exceeding care, as if the painter had determined to crown his labours and honour Seville with a masterpiece."[1]

In the Prado are eight pictures by Cano; the best of these are a " Dead Christ " supported by an angel ; a St. Jerome listening to an angel blowing a trumpet to announce the " Last Judgment," and St. John the Evangelist writing the Apocalypse on the Isle of Patmos.

Of the school of Cano were Alonso de Mesa, Miguel Geronimo Cieza, Don Sebastian di Herrera Barnueva, Pedro Anastasio Bocanegra, Ambrosio Martinez, Sebastian Gomez, and Don Niño de Guevara.

---

[1] Stirling-Maxwell, pp. 802, 803.

PORTRAIT, COUNT OF BENAVENTE.   VELAZQUEZ.   MUSEO DEL PRADO.

VII.

VELAZQUEZ.

It is to the greatest name in this great age of Spanish art that we now turn. In whatever light we regard Velazquez, whether as the painter who led the van in the progress of national art, or as the mind which made that art a large knowledge, and became the teacher of truth to his own and to all times, in the intrinsic grandeur of his character he stands—" Painter of kings, and king of Spanish painters "—by a right which no royal patron confers—but by the will of God. It would be impossible to give more than a meagre outline of such a life. But if we can show the marked qualities of mind that made him the teacher of that age, the general features of his thought as it shaped its art, we shall have done somewhat to our purpose.

The connection of his biography with the whole development of the time concentrates our interest. He is in himself the epitome of its mental and moral history. In one like Murillo we would fain study more the person himself, the inner life of love that lies hid like a well in the desert. But there are a few whose personal activity flows like a tide through the large channel of their time, of whom it is

hard to say whether they more shape it or are shaped by it;
at once the gathered wave of its tendencies, working with
it in their movement, yet only because their individual
powers find there a real path of action.   There is nothing
sporadic in the appearance of such minds.   They come
at the very hour when the world needs them, as states-
men, teachers, reformers, artists.   It is always in the great
transition periods that they arise, when new ideas are
fermenting in the social thought, and men are seeking an
inspired leader—such men, to pass by other instances, appear at times in the history of art.   Michael Angelo was
thus the shaping mind of the Renaissance ; Raffaelle and
Albrecht Dürer were such men ; Velazquez was such a
man.   We may truly class him among the originating
minds who have struck out a new path of thought or action.   As an ideal painter he cannot rank at all with the
master intellects—a Michael Angelo, a Lionardo, a
Titian, a Raffaelle.   He was a very honest, real painter,
who spoke all he knew ; and he knew the truth of nature.

But to know rightly the character of this artist we must
look back at the point where he appears in Spanish art.
It was no longer the dawn of the Renaissance.   The art of
Spain was highly developed ; yet it had been hitherto
little else than a development after Italian models.   It
must pass to its second stage as distinctly national, yet
an art for the world.   New capacities and new needs
began to enlarge its horizon.   It must on one hand keep
its historical union with the truth of the past, yet the

ripened fruit must drop its sombre Spanish husk; it must enter on its noble career; it must receive into itself and transform a foreign civilization. Already the Spanish painters had caught a glimpse of the future; but their training could not fit them to guide it. El Mudo was a noble Spanish artist, but no more. El Greco stumbled at colour; he was suited for gloomy grandeur, but had no large views of historic art. But there was wanted a sinewy intellect, trained in a large culture to educate and guide this new life; and it came in Velazquez.

We are now at a point from which we can rightly trace the steps of his early history.

Diego de Silva Velazquez was born at Seville in 1599, of Portuguese origin. His father had married and settled in Seville, where he was a thriving lawyer. The son was brought up in the usual mode of Spanish society, with an excellent scholastic training, especially in languages and philosophy. But he early manifested that artistic talent; the keen eye and rapid pencil marked the man. At thirteen he entered the school of the elder Herrera, whose harsh temper and rough treatment soon drove him thence. The ground ideas of his method and treatment are to be found in his pupil's works, though the rough bold style has developed into a higher quality of touch and intention.

On leaving Herrera, Velazquez entered the studio of Francisco Pacheco, where he found a quiet home and thorough instruction in academical rules, and the regulations of the Inquisition. But he learned other lessons also, though not from Pacheco—that true art is the most real of things, and nature the best master. "He kept," says Pacheco, "an apprentice, a peasant lad, who served him for a model in different actions and postures; sometimes crying, sometimes laughing, till he had conquered all difficulty in expression." From him he learned to execute every variety of head, drawing them in charcoal or chalk on blue paper, and thus he acquired certainty in likenesses; this was the beginning of his excellence as a portrait-painter. In after days, when critics wished to disparage his work, while admitting his thorough ability in taking likenesses, they said he could paint nothing but head. On Philip IV. repeating this remark to Velazquez, he said they flattered him; for his own part, he knew no one of whom he could say that they painted heads thoroughly well. This story shows us the man. He was a *Naturalist.* He early gained skill in colour by painting fish, fruit, and other objects of still-life. These *Bodegones* are very rare.

Velazquez's life, from the time when he began to devote himself fully to artistic pursuits, was a life spent in hard work. His study was man, and he delighted to mingle with men and to read the problems of art in the actual world,—in the shop of the artisan and the crowds of the market-place, where at every turn he met water-carriers, donkeys, and Sancho Panzas, grave hidalgos in rusty cloaks, and beggars in patches such as even Moscow cannot boast of.

He now studied the manner of Caravaggio and Ribera, and we see their influence on his work in the prevailing sombre tone and strong contrast of light and shade, the hard and defined outline, breadth in handling, correct drawing, and careful composition; but, throughout, the purely *naturalistic* treatment and restriction to common life. To this period belong the "Adoration of the Shepherds," in the Prado, and *el Aguador de Sevilla*—the "Water-Carrier," now at Apsley House.

It was about this time that he married Juana, his master's daughter. Pacheco says of this marriage: "Diego de Sylva Velazquez, my son-in-law, properly occupies the third place, to whom, after five years of education and instruction, I gave my daughter in marriage, moved by his virtue, his purity, and his good parts, as well as by the hope derived from his great natural genius. It is a greater honour to be his master than his father-in-law, and it is, therefore, just to overthrow the boldness of a certain person who desires to claim this glory; taking from me the crown of my declining years. I hold it to be no disgrace for the disciple to surpass his master: Lionardo da Vinci lost nothing by having Raffaelle for a disciple; nor Jorge de Castelfranco (Giorgione), Titian; nor Plato, Aristotle."

Soon after this, at the age of twenty-three, Velazquez left Seville for the purpose of studying the works of Luis Tristan, whose teaching made more impress on his work than any other master at Madrid. He was cordially welcomed there by Don Luis and Don Melchior del Alcazar, of Seville, and also by Don Juan de Fonseca, a courtier and a fellow-countryman.

Before returning to Seville he painted, at Pacheco's request, a portrait of the poet Gongora, which " represents the boasted lyrist of Andalusia as a grave, bald-headed priest of middle age, and more likely to be taken for an inquisitor, jealous of all novelty and freedom of thought, than for a fashionable writer of extravagant conceits, and the leader of a new school of poetry." [1]

Velazquez was recalled a few months later to Madrid. His first work executed there was a portrait of Fonseca, through whom he had received his summons from the Conde-duque de Olivarez. The likeness was so marvellous that at one stride the artist gained the foremost rank. The king himself now sat to him ; again his skill did not fail Velazquez: the portrait was so true to life that Olivarez declared no one had ever painted the king before. At this time Velazquez also made a sketch of Charles I., who was then at Madrid.

The painter was now appointed *Pintor da Camara* (painter in ordinary), with a salary of twenty ducats a month and the honour of being alone privileged to paint the king.

In 1627, Palomino says, he completed a great picture of " the expulsion of the Moriscos by the pious King Philip III., a chastisement well merited by such an infamous and seditious race ; since, faithless to God and to

[1] Stirling-Maxwell, II., p. 588.

the king, they remained obstinate in the sect of Mahomet
and kept up a secret intelligence with the Turks and
Moors of Barbary, with a rebellious intention." Velazquez painted this work in competition with Eugenio
Caxes, Vicente Carducho, and Angelo Nardi, and was
awarded the prize—the post of Usher to the Royal
Chamber—by the judges, Mayno and Crescenzi.

Velazquez was now *Ugier de Camara*, with increased
salary. He painted about this time his picture of " Los
Borrachos," or " Los Bebedores " (The Drinkers), a wonderful group. In the centre a young peasant, seated on a
wine-cask and crowned with vine-leaves, initiates a novice
into the Bacchic rites; around them are gathered their
boon companions, one holding a brimming bowl, another
leaning against him, with a broad grin on his face ; while
the others watch the mystic ceremony. The group of
revellers is unsurpassed in force and breadth of handling.
It has all the brown, sombre hue of Velazquez's earlier
manner, and the colour has grown darker than when
first painted.

In 1628 occurred Rubens's second visit to Madrid.
" With painters," says Pacheco, " he had little inter-
course; only with Don Diego Velazquez (with whom he
had corresponded before), he formed an intimate friendship, and favoured his works because of his great virtue
and modesty ; they visited the Escorial together."

It is probably owing to Rubens's influence that Velazquez sought the king's permission to visit Italy during

the next year. Having gained a reluctant consent, he went first to Venice, where he passed some time in study ; then on to Rome. He was lodged, on his arrival, at the Vatican, where he made a careful study of Michael Angelo and Raffaelle. He was also awhile at the Villa Medici, absorbed in his first real acquaintance with classic art. It was during this Roman visit that he painted "Joseph's Coat," now at the Escorial, and the "Forge of Vulcan," in the Prado. They show little trace of his study of the antique. ·There is a freer handling in the "Forge of the Vulcan" than in his earlier works, and fewer heavy, dark shadows; the figures stand out from the canvas in flesh and blood. They are marvellously real ; but they are common men, not ideal gods.

It has been said that a man has no new thought after thirty. There is truth in this, but only a half truth. If it be meant at all that the most vigorous intellect belongs to the earlier years, nothing can be falser. There is a stage in the green corn, when the ear is larger than in its ripeness, but distended and empty; a rich intellect like Velazquez has, too, its time of luxuriance until about thirty, and then it turns within to gain fulness and natural strength. The season which yields the most complete intellectual results is often from thirty to fifty.

Velazquez was no exception to this natural law. We see a steady growth in his work after his Italian journey, but no abrupt change of manner. There are a greater warmth and transparency of colour, few contrasting tints, less heavy shadow and hard outline, and a softer background. The grey tints of his later pictures replace the sombre brown tone of "los Borrachos." His colour shows plainly the influence of Rubens and the Venetian masters; and his study of the antique appears in his careful modelling. But he is still the simple copier of nature, whether his tone be silvery-grey or sombre brown. His study of ideal art has but taught him to be more real.

Perhaps the truest attainment in style is when we learn simply to speak our thoughts, and let them find their own expression. A young painter is apt, like a young writer, to put himself into an attitude and to search after strong contrasts and illustrations. But a Velazquez soon learns that his true aim is to utter his ideas clearly and fully, and his imagination and feeling will blend with his logic. He is the most elaborate of painters, great in his use and great in his rejection of colour, yet we may always see in his most splendid compositions a plain line of argument. It is the forgetfulness of this law of true speech which begets inflation for fulness, affectation for real grace, and weakness for strength. It seems the easiest, yet it is the hardest thing to be natural.

Velazquez's first work, on his return from Italy, was a portrait of the infant Prince Baltasar Carlos; this work no longer exists. It is to a later period that we owe those charming pictures of the gallant, bright-faced boy who comes so often before us, now on his bay pony, now in

hunting-dress with his dogs beside him.   The artist's
whole time was occupied in painting the king, the different members of the royal family, and the grandees of
the court.   Among these numerous portraits is one of
Philip on horseback, and a magnificent picture of Olivarez, one of the most striking portraits ever painted by
Velazquez.

In 1639 Velazquez painted the noble Crucifixion, now
at Madrid, for the Convent of San Placido.   It has not
the dim landscape, or the background of lowering clouds
usual in pictures of the crucifixion.   It is sternly simple ;
it has all the grandeur of sculpture.   The calmness of
death lifts us above the thought of Christ's suffering.
There is a strange melancholy which the grandest works
of art sometimes beget in us, especially if we view them
while we ourselves are in the midst of lofty but unfinished
labours.   A statue, a painting seem no longer human ; they
are disengaged from all past processes of imperfection ;
they have passed from the stage of becoming to the state
of changeless being.   We see no more the struggling
artist, but, as it were, an instant creation.   Their completeness withers our hope.   The scaffolding on which
a Velazquez stood is gone, and the lofty painting looks
down on us with an overwhelming grandeur, an unattain-
able distance.

About the same time Velazquez painted a portait of the
Admiral Adrian Pulido Pareja.   This work recalls forcibly the style of Herrera, being painted with large brushes,

CRUCIFIXION. VELAZQUEZ. MUSEO DEL PRADO.

in a free, bold manner, and if looked at too closely it seems a mass of blotchy colours. Palomino tells us that Philip IV., on entering the painter's studio and seeing this picture before him, exclaimed: "Still here; you have received your orders, why have you not gone?" On discovering his mistake the king turned toward Velazquez and said: " I assure you I was deceived." To this period belong also his admirable pictures of the "Bobo de Coria," the "Niño de Vallecas," and several other dwarfs. In 1644 Velazquez painted an equestrian portrait of the Queen Isabella, a companion piece to the picture of Philip IV., executed eighteen years earlier.

A few years later Velazquez painted the king, armed and on horseback. But the portrait met with general disapproval, among other things, the horse being, said the critics, contrary to all rules of art. Vexed with the adverse criticism the artist painted out the greater portion of his work, inscribing at the same time on the canvas: "*Didacus Velazquius, Pictor expinsit.*"

1647 is the date of the "Surrender of Breda," commonly called "Las Lanzas," from the line of soldiers with uplifted pikes behind the Marquis of Spinola, who, with gracious dignity, receives the keys from Prince Justin of Nassau. At the left of the picture stands a figure in grey, with a slouched hat and feather, a dark, handsome face, probably the artist's own portrait.

In 1648 Velazquez was sent to Italy to collect works of art for an academy, which the king had long wished to

found in Madrid. He sailed from Malaga in November,
and landing at Genoa, passed hurriedly through Milan
and Padua to Venice, where he purchased several pictures, among which were Tintoretto's "Israelites Gathering Manna," the "Conversion of St. Paul," and "Glory
of Heaven," a sketch of his great picture, and a Venus
and Adonis by Paul Veronese. In Boschini's singular
poem, in the Venetian dialect, entitled "La Carta de
Navegar Pitoresco," is an account of a conversation held
later in Rome between Salvator Rosa and Velazquez.
The latter was asked his opinion of Raffaelle:

> Lu storse el cao cirimoniosamente,
> E disse : " Rafael (a dirve el vero ;
> Piasendome esser libero, e sinciero)
> Stago per dir, che nol me piase niente."

> " Tanto che (repliché quela persona)
> Co'no ve piase questo gran Pitor ;
> In Italia nissun ve dà in l' umor ;
> Perche nu ghe donemo la Corona ;"

> Don Diego repliché con tal maniera :
> " A Venetia se trova el bon, e'l belo ;
> Mi dago el primo liogo a quel penelo ;
> Tician xe quel, che porta la bandiera." [1]

[1] Proudly the Master turned his head :
"In Raffaelle forsooth," he said,
" (You know I always speak my mind,)
No wondrous aptitude I find."

"Nay," said the other, "if indeed
To Raffaelle you refuse the meed,
Whom do you find in Italy
More worthy of the crown than he ?"

" In Venice," quoth Diego, "where
Who seeks shall find both good and fair,
Titian is over all men lord—
To him the banner I award."

After his visit at Venice Velazquez stopped awhile at Bologna, Parma, and Florence, and then hastened through Rome to Naples. Having arranged the object of his journey with the viceroy, Count Oñate, and renewed his acquaintance with Ribera, he returned to Rome. While there he executed the superb portrait of Pope Innocent X., now in the Doria Pamphili Palace, and which is the only real specimen of his art now in Rome. We have but meagre details of this Italian visit; we only know that Velazquez returned to Spain in 1651, leaving his large collection of works of art to be brought to Madrid in the following year by the Count Oñate.

On his arrival at the capital Velazquez was appointed *Aposentador Mayor*, or Royal Quarter Master, a position which the architects Herrera and Moya had held under Philip II. It was a place of great importance, giving much influence to the artist, and bringing him into constant contact with the king. He had general oversight of all public festivals, and a certain jurisdiction within the palace. Velazquez applied for this office, feeling his peculiar fitness for the post; accustomed as he was to superintend the decoration of the palace, and versed in all the details of court etiquette. The rest of his life was spent in the duties of his office, duties which Palomino tells us required the entire time and attention of the officer, and which, therefore, were the last to have devolved on Velazquez; they have robbed the world of many noble works.

In 1660 Velazquez left Madrid to superintend the arrangements made for the meeting of the Spanish and French monarchs on the banks of the Bidassoa, where the Infanta Maria Teresa was married to the French king. It is supposed that the fatigue and exposure undergone by Velazquez during these court ceremonials were the cause of his death, which occurred on August 7, 1660, after a week's illness. He was in his sixty-second year.

Much as we must mourn the loss to art which this busy court life of Velazquez made needful, yet we owe to this very period some of his finest works. It was then that he painted his masterpiece "Las Hilanderas" (the tapestry weavers). In a large room in the royal tapestry manufactory of Santa Isabel are a group of women at work. In the foreground is an old woman at her spinning-wheel; she turns her head to speak to a young girl behind her, who is drawing back a red curtain. In the centre a girl dressed in scarlet stops her carding to watch a sleeping cat. Near her sits a woman in a green gown, winding yarn from a reel; behind her stands a girl holding a basket. In the background is an alcove in which we see three ladies looking at a piece of tapestry.

This picture has all the marvellous blending of colour of Velazquez's later works: a soft and rounded outline, great transparency of tone, simple handling, and great breadth of treatment. Raphael Mengs says it is "rather the result of his will than work of his hands."

In 1656 Velazquez painted "Las Meniñas" (the maids

of honour). In the centre of a long room stands the little
Infanta Margarita Maria, a pleasing, fair-haired child, with
the full Austrian cheek and hanging lip. A kneeling
Meniña hands her a cup of water; at her left hand
another is dropping a low courtesy. In the foreground
stand the dwarfs Mari Barbola and Nicolas Pertusato, the
latter of whom is worrying with his foot a patient, tawny
hound. On the left side stands Velazquez at his easel
painting the portraits of the king and queen, whose heads
are reflected in a mirror, while in the background are
two ladies talking; behind them is an open door, through
which we see the *Aposentador del Reyna* mounting a staircase. The room is hung with pictures, and lighted by
three windows. No Dutch interior ever surpassed the
finish of this work. Wilkie says: " He (Velazquez) is
Teniers on a large scale; his handling is of the most
sparkling kind, owing much of its dazzling effect to the
flatness of the ground it is placed upon. The picture of
children in grotesque dresses in his painting-room is a
surprising piece of handling." ' There is a story that the
king on seeing this picture said there was but one thing
lacking in it, and painted the cross of Santiago on the
artist's breast with his own hand. Giordano called it *la
teologia de la pintura.*

It is in Madrid that Velazquez must be studied. The
Prado possesses sixty of his pictures; and there the
mighty painter may be seen in all his splendour, in por-

' Cunningham's " Life of Wilkie," II., p. 488.

trait, historical paintings, in *genre* pictures, in landscape.
For Velazquez was the first and greatest landscape-painter
of Spain.   Wilkie says of him: "Velazquez is the only
Spanish painter who seems to have made an attempt at
landscape; I have seen some of his most original and
daring.   Titian seems to be his model; and although he
lived before the time of Claude and Salvator Rosa, he
appears to have combined the breadth and picturesque
effect for which these two great painters are remarkable."[1]   Again, he writes to Collins: "Much as I might
learn from Spain and from her arts, you, as a landscape-
painter, could learn but little, excepting only some works
by Velazquez, who in landscape is a brilliant exception to
the Spanish school.   Of him I saw a rich landscape at
Madrid that for breadth and richness I have seldom seen
equalled.   * * *   It was too abstract to have much
detail or imitation; but it had the very sun we see, and
the air we breathe—the very soul and spirit of nature."[2]

There are nine landscapes by Velazquez in the Prado.
One of the finest is the picture of "St. Paul and St.
Anthony Fed by a Raven in the Desert."   It is of this
which Wilkie possibly speaks.   His landscapes are rather
in his second manner; the background often too blue,
and therefore monotonous, but his pictures are original
and unconventional: he takes in the world of nature and
blends on the canvas the changeful hues of the landscape

[1] Cunningham's "Life of Wilkie," II., p. 519.
[2] Cunningham's "Life of Wilkie," II., p. 524.

ST. ANTHONY AND ST. PAUL IN THE DESERT. VELAZQUEZ. MUSEO DEL PRADO

and the form of living men as few artists have done; he
speaks in the language of Nature herself, in light, form,
and colour; he shows his power in his marvellous tints and
those varied greys which characterize so much of his work.

The charm of Velazquez is the infinite variety of light
and shade, the grotesque mingling of great and small, of
prince and fool, Philip IV. and El Niño de Vallecas. It
is life rather than art that he shows us. You saunter with
him along a noisy market-place, where the women are
selling fruit and flowers, and the beggars beggar description; and suddenly you turn into some cool, quiet street,
where there is no sign of life save an old woman knitting
at a latticed window, or a child playing near a stone fountain. You pass under some tall archway decorated with
some half-crumbling sculptures, and you stand in the
court of an old palace, and gaze upon odd mis-
shapen dwarfs or the richly dressed nobles. Every object
you meet on his canvas is real. Here comes a water-
carrier with his earthen jar; and here El Bobo de Coria
with his look of spiteful cunning; there the little prince
Baltasar Carlos dashes by on his bay pony, and behind
him gleam the snow-peaks of the Sierra; and here stares
forth a fine lady in her rouge and wondrous frizzed hair.
From My Lord Duke to the beggar his canvas is crowded
with all classes. We see the men before us in flesh and
blood; they are ready to walk out of their frames; we
can hear them speak. His magic pencil writes the mind
on the face. It is the real record history of men.

These are but a few gems from this treasure-house of

the Prado, but they show the man. In the great name of Velazquez we have that which attracts us beyond all else. It is the power of that biography that it does not give us merely the picture of a court etiquette, a personage decorated and robed for state occasions; but the human nature which all the costume cannot hide. It is not a character of severe simplicity, like that of a Juanes. It belongs to a day of courtlier refinement. He is the splendid painter, who loves the feast and the court. Yet with all this, when we look at that brilliant life, we see a true type of the wise and good and noble artist. We see in him that true etiquette which is not merely the " ornamental border of society," which is not on the surface, but is the form in which the beauty of the social nature expresses itself; the flowers and figures inwrought with the tissue of a fine tapestry that cannot be torn away without destroying the web. There are few characters more drawn to the life; we can hardly image a better one than is given in that history of his time—his own works. In them you have at once the man, the courtier, the student of nature, the artist.

There is, indeed, hardly a painter, whose personal character stands out more boldly from the canvas than his. His individuality is etched in every line. We see his very look and manner in " Las Lanzas " and " Las Meniñas." He is no shadow, but a genuine man, with the marked qualities of his own peculiar temperament and its defects also. We image him as a slight, nervous, active person, with great grace of manner and magnetism of look, of earnest speech that controlled all who came within his speech; impetuous at times, resolute, but always generous, brave, affectionate; a man who made strong friends and strong enemies. None is more large-hearted than he toward poorer artists. There is a refined courtesy in him, whether he speaks to a Rubens or helps on a young Murillo. There is a tenderness in his home-life, which beats with all the pulses of his heart. It is the man we feel everywhere; the intellect, the culture, but warmed by the affections, and blended with the ripe, compact strength of the great artist.

We are thus to study him as a reality. A great man is almost always a myth to the after-world. We look at him as we do at a polished statue, the finished work of the chisel, and can hardly feel that it has gone through the long, real processes of toil, but it seems to have stepped forth in beauty from the stone. Fortunately for us the character of Velazquez has been preserved, and we know him in each stroke of his pencil and dip of his brush on the palette. The character of the man is the character of his paintings. They are the simple living portraiture of common life. Velazquez stands the noblest type of Spanish art. Nor did he wait till after death for fame—*pintor da Camara, Ugier de camara, ayuda de la guarda ropa, Aposentador Mayor*; the intimate friend of Philip II., decorated with the cross of Santiago, honoured by all great and small—his apotheosis came while he was yet alive. Here he is a name; in Spain he was a reality.

VIII.

MURILLO.

WHETHER a great man makes his age or his age makes him, has long been a controversy, but certainly a mistaken one. A human intellect does not grow up *in vacuo* as a plant grows under a glass. A pine tree and a plantain are the product of their respective climates, and genius takes its shape and development from the circumstances of an age and a people. Murillo could have flourished only in Spain, and there only at the time when the domination of the Renaissance had ceased, and for the first time there was possible a distinctively Spanish art. The discussions about originality of genius are mere words. A genius, absolutely self fed, is impossible; for every mind is a debtor to nature and kindred mind. But the real difference between originality and mere second-hand intellect is, that true genius assimilates without losing its own identity. The master sees in Titian what is not Titian but beauty apart from him, the common inspiration of all lovers of beauty; the imitator only studies the trick of Titian's handling, and becomes a good copyist. Each new genius is its own archetype.

Murillo is the painter of sentiment,—a genius by no

EDUCATION OF THE VIRGIN. MURILLO. MUSEO DEL PRADO.

means so original as Velazquez, but with that mild, gentle spirit which bathes every thing in its own soft light. We shall not err when we say that Murillo is the sweetest and richest painter of his day. We love him in spite of faults, and we find morsels of his painting a daily feast. He has a glowing fancy, eye for all beauty of nature and life, and a lofty mind and moral purpose. His magic pencil writes the heart of his saints on the face; none better than he can draw the pure brow of childhood; and, above all, his conceptions suggest a mystery hidden beneath the outward colouring.

His name recalls Spanish art in the noon of its glory. There is in that series of great and small artists, not one who has so won the heart of all time; none depicts so much of that personal beauty which gives life to the past. We approach Zurbaran with somewhat of awe; Velazquez is the grand historical painter. But in Murillo we see the mingling of the two, with a milder grace. In him we see the sweet singer with the golden harp strung always before him,—the man with all the chords of his fine nature touched by the Holy Ghost. His life is no historic poem like that of Velazquez, which brings before us all the scenes of national pride—its battles and its social triumphs, its court, its festivals, its long years of intrigue and etiquette.

Murillo's life was the quiet, uneventful career of a simple painter. Born at Seville in 1617, his early years were passed in his humble home amidst his studies. At his parents' death he was apprenticed to the painter Juan del Castillo, a pupil of Luis Fernandez. His master trained him for a correct draughtsman, drilling him also in the mechanical part of his work, in cleaning brushes, grinding colours, and such wearisome tasks. Murillo was an apt and diligent scholar. He soon learned all that the master could teach him. In 1640 Castillo removed to Cadiz, leaving his pupil to follow his art at Seville. Murillo painted at this time pictures for sale at the *Feria*, or weekly market. It is probable that he owed to this rapid work much of the freedom of touch which is so prominent a feature in his painting. To this period belong the " Virgin with St. Francis," painted for the Convent *de Regina*,—a hard, flat work, in Castillo's dry manner ; and the " Virgin del Rosario " with San Domingo, executed for the Colegio di Santo Tomas. Of the latter picture, Head says : " In the angels' heads Murillo has evidently imitated Roelas, and there are about some of them glimpses of his later style. The face of the Virgin is very beautiful, and her drapery, though rather angular in its folds, well painted. The picture is signed ' Bar^{meus} Murillo. "

But it was time that the next step in the education of the artist should come ; that he should look beyond his common subjects to classic types of beauty, and to the living ideal. His fellow-student in Castillo's studio— Pedro de Moya—returned, in 1642, to Seville, having studied under Van Dyck. He brought with him copies

of that painter's works, and other gems of Flemish art.
The study of these pictures roused Murillo to a sense of
his need of instruction. He hastened to prepare for a
journey to Rome. He bought a square of coarse canvas
and cut it into several pieces, on which he painted rapid
sketches which were easily sold, thus enabling him to pro-
vide for his sister and for his own simple needs. He
started on foot over the Sierras, arriving in Madrid without money or friends. He sought out Velazquez, then in
the zenith of his fame. The great painter received him
cordially, taking him to his own house, and persuading
him to remain at Madrid and to devote himself to careful
study of the great masters in the Escorial and Buenretiro. Murillo was, above all, attracted by Van Dyck,
Ribera, and Velazquez. He copied many of their pictures, and soon made marvellous progress in the use of
colour and freedom of handling. His progress awoke
wonder and admiration in Velazquez and all who watched
him. It was the result of a long preparation; the intellectual energy, the fervour of heart, the correct eye, the
rapid pencil of the painter only needed a new aim. The
influence of the great masters affected him like the drop
which falls into the liquid that is just ready for crystalli-
zation. Almost at a touch his faculties took form; Murillo became the noble and powerful artist.

Murillo returned to Seville in 1645; and in the following year began a series of pictures for the convent of San
Francisco. These are painted in what is called his first

or "cold" manner (*frio*), with the clear and decided outline, strongly marked shadows and broad handling, which recall Ribera and Zurbaran. The first of the series represents St. Francis lying on an iron pallet and listening entranced to an angel playing on a violin. In another we see St. Diego blessing a pot of broth, before giving it to the beggars who surround him. The death of St. Clara is the noblest of the pictures. The "Angel Kitchen" in the Louvre, and the "Ecstasy of St. Giles," belong also to this series.

And here at once the artist's career opened before him. We must run rapidly over it, and only sum its main features. From every side work poured in on him. The Holy Family with the bird, *del Pajarito*, the "Adoration of the Shepherds," "Rebecca and Eliezer," now in the Prado, were probably painted within the next few years, as were also the jolly sun-burnt beggar-boys that we meet elsewhere on Murillo's canvas, but no specimens of which remain in Spain. In these pictures we find his second or "warm" (*calido*) manner.

In 1648 Murillo married the rich and noble Doña Beatriz de Cabrera y Sotomayo. We know little of his domestic life. His elder son, Gaspar Esteban, emigrated to America; the younger, Gabriel Esteban, imitated his father, and eventually became a canon in the Cathedral of Seville. His daughter Francisca became a nun. After his marriage Murillo adopted the softer and more mellow colouring which we find in his best works; although at no

time can we mark the transition from one style to another.
Several of his later works are in the *calido* manner; indeed
Viardot supposes that he kept the *frio* for scenes of low
life, while for the ecstasies of saints he used the *calido*, and
painted in the *vaporoso* his Annunciations and Conceptions, and the Child Jesus. From this time the artist's
brush was never at rest. We must, however, content ourselves with mentioning a few of his leading works. In
1652 Murillo painted Our Lady of the Conception for the
brethren of the true cross; and in 1655 Don Juan Fed-
erighi of Carmona commissioned him to paint for the
sacristy of the cathedral the pictures of St. Leander and
St. Isidore. The latter is a portrait of the licentiate Juan
Lopez de Talaban, a stern, vigorous figure, a fine contrast
to the mild, benignant St. Leander, a portrait of Alonso
de Herrera, marker of the choir. In the same year were
painted the pictures of Sta. Maria la Blanca; they were
carried to Paris by Marshal Soult, but the larger works
were brought to Madrid with the St. Elizabeth, and now
hang in the Academy of San Fernando. They represent
the " Dream of the Roman Senator and his Wife,"—the
legend connected with the building of Sta. Maria Mag-
giore. In the first picture, The Dream, the Senator is
asleep in his chair; his wife is lying on the floor; he sees
the vision of the Madonna with the child in her arms; she
points to the distant hill where he shall build the church.
In the second picture, the Senator relates his dream to
the Pope. The Dream is painted in Murillo's third man-

ner, the *vaporoso*. The other pictures were not recovered from the French, but were sold in the Soult collection ; one, a Conception, is now in the Louvre. In the following year Murillo executed the " St. Anthony of Padua Receiving the Infant Christ," now in the cathedral at Seville.

Murillo long endeavoured to establish a public academy of painting at Seville. It was a weary work to overcome the indifference and jealousy of other painters. But at last his work was crowned with success. The society met for the first time on the first of January, 1660, and drew up a simple constitution, by which each pupil on admission was obliged to declare that—" Praised be the most holy Sacrament and the pure conception of our Lady," *Alabado sea el Santisimo Sacramento y limpià Concepcion de Nuestra Señora.* Swearing, and all misconduct, were punished by fines. The instruction was meant for art students who desired a thorough course of study from life ; but after the first years when Murillo was at the head, the arrogance of Valdés Leal and constant rivalry among the members dwarfed its power. Its last official record is the minutes of a meeting held in 1673. We see but little trace of the influence of the Seville Academy on Spanish art, yet it may have helped stem its decay. After the second year Murillo gave up all connection with the Academy, devoting himself to his ever-increasing work, and to the pupils in his own studio. We owe to this period the " Virgin of the Conception," and the eight half-length pictures of saints, still preserved in the cathedral.

We now approach the noblest monument of his genius and of the Christianity of his time. For many years there had existed at Seville the Brotherhood of the Holy Charity, who had built the Hospital of San Jorge. But the hospital was now in ruins, and the guild in great poverty. In 1661 Don Miguel Mañara Vicentelo de Leca, a noble knight and member of the guild, vowed to rebuild the hospital.

In this age of cold neglect, he woke all Seville into religious life, and completed this noble work of his love to Christ. Its corner-stone was the life-savings of a poor beggar called Luis; on this rose the noble Church of San Jorge, with its rich altars and lofty walls, whence the faces of angels and saints look down upon the devout worshipper, and the hospital with its marble cloisters and grand halls, where the faithful priests and sisters of mercy lavish tender care on " their masters and lords the poor."

The church is a huge pile in Greco-Roman style, with little grandeur or grace. The interior is fine ; a single aisle crowned with a lofty dome ; at the end the rich altar, a superb piece of massive gilding. For this church Murillo painted eleven pictures ; three—the " Annunciation," the " Infant Saviour," and the " Infant St. John,"— still hang in their place above the side altars. The remaining eight are Murillo's master-work. On either side of the church originally hung four of the pictures. On the left, " Moses Striking the Rock," the " Return of the Prodigal," " Abraham Receiving the Three Angels," and

the " Charity of San Juan de Dios "; and on the right,
the " Miracle of the Loaves and Fishes," " Our Lord Heal-
ing the Paralytic at the Pool of Bethesda," " St. Peter Re-
leased from Prison by the Angel," and " St. Elizabeth of
Hungary." Marshal Soult carried off four of these pictures—Abraham Receiving the Angels, the Prodigal Son,
St. Peter and the Angel, and the Pool of Bethesda ; and
the two first are now in the collection of the Duke of
Sutherland. Wilkie says of these : " They are light pictures compared with the series they belonged to in the
' Caridad ' ; have skies for backgrounds ; still, the " Return
of the Prodigal Son " is an impressive picture, having this
quality of simple homeliness in common with many of the
figures of Raphael and Rembrandt, that they seem as if
speaking the very language of Scripture." [1] It is the un-
quenched yearning of the human heart that we see, as
the prodigal falls at his father's feet. In the background stand servants bearing the ring and the " best
robe " ; on the left is a boy leading the " fatted calf,"
while a little white dog fawns on the wanderer.

" Moses Striking the Rock" and the " Miracle of the
Loaves and Fishes," are still in the *Caridad*. They have
little of Murillo's usual brilliancy of colour, and the treatment is light and sketchy. In the former, commonly called
La Sed, Moses stands by the rock in Horeb, from which
the water pours ; by his side is Aaron, then, as always, the
type of the priest, not the statesman ; and around him

---

[1] Cunningham's " Life of Wilkie," III., p. 117.

press the eager, thirsty people. Each stroke is of a master-hand: the woman, who in her burning thirst forgets her babe; the strong men, who, kneeling by the stream, drink from the hollow of the hand; the sheep and dogs who crowd by them toward the water; the patient camel waiting his turn; the heavy-laden mule who drinks from an iron pot;—all is drawn to the life. The sun-burnt boy on the mule, and the girl near him, are perhaps the painter's own children. In strong contrast to the common people is the lofty figure of Moses. He is not here, as the genius of Angelo carved him, the stern Law-giver, sitting alone, colossal, his hand grasping the tables of stone, his furrowed brow lifted as if he saw the vision of a Divine State; it is rather the "meekest of men," who prays God that his sinning people may be spared; "and if not—blot me, I pray Thee, out of Thy book"—it is this face that is raised in gratitude to Jehovah.

The "Loaves and Fishes" is not equal to the Moses, though treated in the same manner.

The "Charity of San Juan de Dios" represents the saint as fainting beneath the weight of a wretched beggar whom be bears on his shoulders; an angel supports San Juan.

On the completion of his work at the *Caridad*, Murillo was employed at the Capuchin Convent just outside the city walls. Seventeen of the pictures then executed are now in the Seville Museum. The greatest of these are the "St. Thomas of Villanueva," the "Vision of St.

Felix," "St. Francis of Assisi," " The Virgin of the Conception," the "Annunciation," "The Virgin with the Dead Christ," and "St. Anthony of Padua." In the Museum is also the *" Virgin de la Servilleta,"* which was painted for a lay brother, the cook of the convent. Having no canvas at hand, Murillo took a coarse napkin and painted on it a matchless Madonna and Child. It is fresh as if painted yesterday. The "St. Thomas of Villanueva" was a favourite subject with Murillo ; there is a fine example in the Louvre and another in England ; but Palomino tells us that Murillo was wont to call the work in the Capuchin Convent *" su lienzo,"* his own picture. St. Thomas stands at the cathedral door, while around him cluster the poor, seeking alms ; the saint's figure is noble and dignified—the beggars are drawn to the life.

The St. Felix of Cantalicio is a marvel of beauty and colour. The saint—an Italian capuchin of the sixteenth century—holds in his arms the Infant Christ, and gazes up at the Virgin, who has just placed the babe in his arms. The beauty and grace of the Virgin are matchless.

The St. Francis is one of the noblest of Murillo's devotional pictures. It represents the appearance of Christ to the saint on Mount Alvernus when he received the *stigmata*. St. Francis stands by the cross ; his left arm is around the bending form of the Saviour, who rests one hand on his shoulder, while he hangs from the cross by the other. There is a charm in it that softens the horror of Calvary, as if a sunbeam had stolen through the eclipse,

IMMACULATE CONCEPTION. MURILLO. MUSEO DEL PRADO.

and rested on the cross and the saint standing beneath it; it is a true blending of the Godhead with humanity, the Saviour's heart yearning with love in the very pangs of death.

The large picture of the Virgin granting to St. Francis the Jubilee of the Porciuncula is now in the Prado. It has been sadly repainted.

Murillo painted two Conceptions for this convent, which are also in the Museum. They are but two of the many marvels he executed in honour of the Immaculate Conception. In the Prado alone are four paintings of this subject, all of great merit, yet we leave them to gaze again and again at one simpler and more youthful than the others. We wander through the halls with their gems of Italian and Flemish art, and we go back from them to sit down with Murillo.

Certainly his portraits of the Holy Child have more of divine and human grace mingled than any thing done by mortal hand. It is real childhood that he pictures in the *Niños Dios*. " The.Good Shepherd " sits with the lamb beside him, with a childlike eye painting the vision of His future life; or as in the still more exquisite picture " Los Niños de la Concha," where the Child Jesus holds a shell filled with water to the little St. John's lips.

We can name here but a few more of his works. He was a noble portrait-painter, and his landscapes are fine, though without the originality of Velazquez. His landscape is merely a background to his figures; the imper-

sonal objects around him only serve to illustrate and fill
up the historic painting. Yet conventional and cold
though they be, their grey tones have a marvellous power
in throwing out the mellow hue of his figures, which
stand forth from the canvas free and detached against
the clear atmosphere.

In the midst of his active labour the artist's hand was
stilled. In 1680, while employed on a painting of the
" Marriage of St. Catharine," tradition says at Cadiz, he
fell from the scaffold, and was seriously injured. He
lingered for some time, passing his hours in prayer in the
Church of Santa Cruz, where hung the " Descent from
the Cross " of Campaña. He died on April 3, 1682, and
was buried at the foot of the picture which he had so
loved.

We find on his canvas the biography of all the scenes
of the market-place, the every-day life of the common
people. In his Holy Families we recall the very image of
his youth ; the earnest, dark-eyed peasant women ; the
sombre Franciscans ; the happy, laughing children. We
breathe everywhere the air of Andalusia ; we look on its
bare hills, the transparent waters, and the valleys that
laugh and sing ; the gayest flowers, the freshest fields, and
the cattle feeding in green nooks ; along the road at every
turn you meet a rough shrine, with a figure of the Virgin
or Christ, and an inscription calling you to prayers. It is
a series of fair pictures it brings before you ; but more
than all we have the purity of a man who, through all the

temptations of an artist's life, has known a higher power
than nature,—whose life is a hymn of faith and love.

There is, perhaps, no point where Murillo appears in
more winning beauty than in his relations with other
painters. He shows the most generous soul, the rarest
gentleness; a heart where the struggles of youth have
only brought forth the richest fruits. We see the picture
of a man too great for little hates. His is a character
shaped by the mild spirit of Christ's religion. He has
heard from those gracious lips: " Blessed are the peace-
makers."

Murillo stands forth as a mind which most faithfully
represents Spanish genius, art, religion; who lived a
Spaniard of the Spaniards in that brilliant world; who
wore the same long cloak and grave dignity as is now
met with in the narrow, dirty lanes of Seville; nay, more,
who had a living human heart, and who pondered as we
now ponder the problems of art and life; who taught a
nation and an age.

It is a mighty step in the history of art, which we have
traced from the first. We image the earlier master as
standing a watchman on the ramparts of the city, and as
his eye gazes through the twilight he sees on the horizon
a dim but coming vision. He describes it as it is to his
eye, with all the familiar colours of the landscape, the hill
and the valley. But this time is the bloom of all that is
richest in art. We have indeed a *Spanish* art, but there
is no other like it.

Velazquez gave the marvellous, complete structure. But Murillo gave much that was harmonious in the finished building. He gave a worship, and we must not undervalue the true power of that visible art in nursing the strong affections of the people, the moral faith, the pure reverence, which to this day make the Sevillian call any noble picture "a Murillo." There is in the noblest painting that "touch of nature which makes the whole world kin." The Infant Christ of Murillo will move the chords of joy and reverence in the most untutored heart as well as in the refined lover of art. It is the same unconscious awe that bows the soul of the peasant with that of the more thoughtful worshipper, when they kneel together beneath the stately arches of a Toledo or a Seville.

Our design has been to sketch the lives and characters of the most eminent of the painters of this time. In itself, indeed, this is a study of most living interest. The personal features of each life give a special charm to the page. We cannot understand two such painters merely by comparing them with each other, although comparisons may furnish a brilliant antithesis. Each is an individual. But they should be studied in their contrasting harmony with each other; and in such a light they throw a rich prismatic ray on the whole character of Spanish art. "Of Velazquez, I do not know how to speak with becoming and sufficient respect. Although his mind did not lead him to depict the perfect types of sublimity, grandeur, and beauty affected by Michael Angelo, Raffaelle, and Leonardo; and although we rarely find in him the glow and fervour of a Titian or a Tintoretto, he seems to me to have been the painter who certainly attained the power of representing all that can be seen in the subject of a picture with greater truth and greater facility than any other artist who ever lived. In the *method* of his picture he realizes perfection, and in his best works there is more solidity where solidity should appear, and more air where air should appear, than I have ever been able to find in the paintings of any other master.

" Murillo, his great rival, had many noble qualities as a painter, and none more transcendent than his power of creating an impression of space and atmosphere. His figures always stand free and detached; they are fully raised and lifted from one another, and from his backgrounds; so that they appear almost as if projected in accordance with the laws of binocular vision." [1]

" For handling no one surpasses him" (Velazquez); " but in colour Reynolds is much beyond him, and so is Murillo. Compared with Murillo, indeed, he has greater talent; was more the founder of a school—more capable of giving a new direction to art; he has displayed the philosophy of art, but Murillo has concealed it, and we are surprised that art and address can do so much. One wonders, too, that sheer simplicity should be so little be-

---

[1] M. Digby Wyatt, " Fine Art," p. 257.

hind them.   In painting an intelligent portrait Velazquez
is nearly unrivalled, but where he attempts simple nature
or sacred subjects, he is far inferior to Murillo."[1]

" Murillo, though of the same school, and of nearly the
same time, is a painter opposed in almost every thing to
Velazquez.   If not greater in point of talent, his subjects
are more elevated, his painting and colouring more general and abstract at the. same time.   While the qualities
of Velazquez are fitted chiefly for the artist, from their
high technical excellence, those of Murillo, from their extreme simplicity, are addressed to the multitude.   No
painter is so universally popular as Murillo; without trick
or vulgar imitation, he attracts every one by his power,
and adapts the higher subjects of art to the commonest
understanding.   Perhaps that very power tells to his
prejudice amongst painters, who suppose the great qualities of art can be appreciated only by the few ; but, unless
art can affect the uninstructed, it loses its influence upon
the great mass of mankind.   As a colourist I should be
disposed to give Murillo a high place ; he is sometimes in
his backgrounds heated and foxy ; but in his flesh he has
an object distinct from most of his contemporaries, and
seems, like Rembrandt, to aim at the general character of
flesh when tinged with the glow of the sun.   His
colour seems adapted for the highest class of art; it is
never minute or particular, but a general and poetical
recollection of nature ; and when successful it is of the

[1] Cunningham's "Life of Wilkie," II., p. 506, Letter to Mr. Phillips.

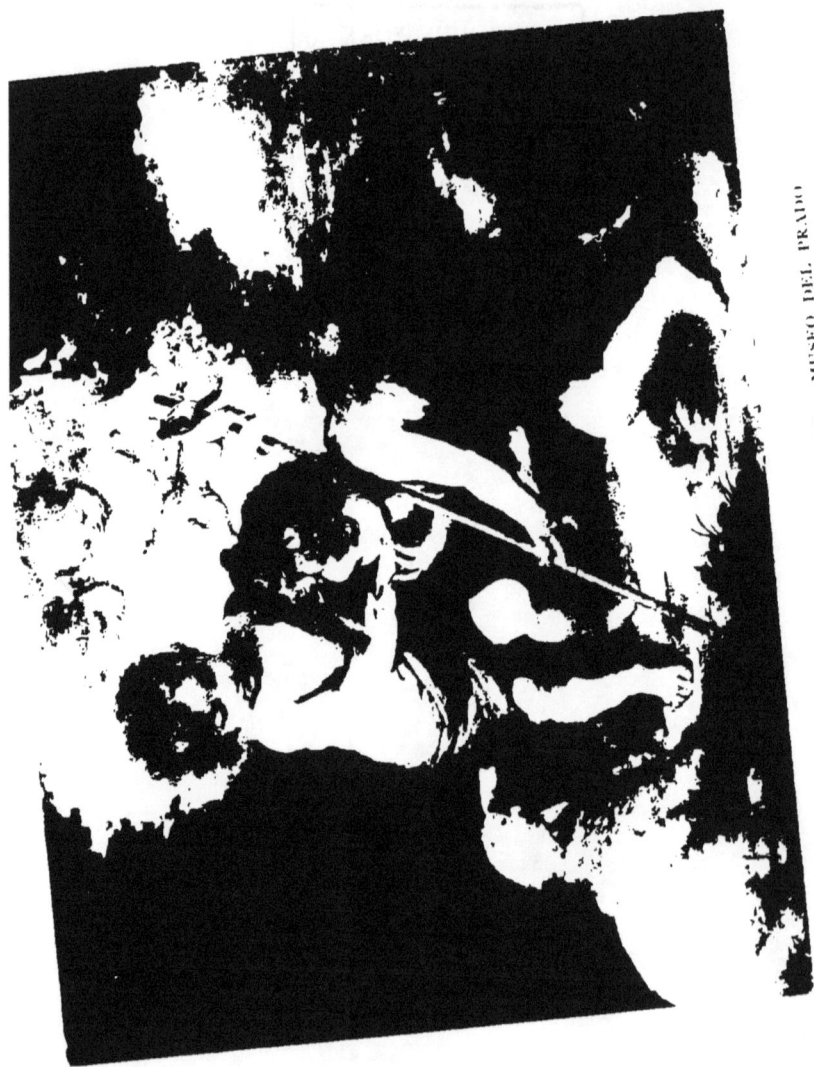

LOS NIÑOS DE LA CONCHA.   MURILLO.   MUSEO DEL PRADO

same class, and, in no remote degree, an approach to Titian and Correggio."[1]

"Velazquez and Murillo are preferred, and preferred with reason, to all the others, as the most original and characteristic of their school. These two great painters are remarkable for having lived in the same time, in the same school, painted from the same people, and of the same age, and yet to have formed two styles so different and opposite, that the most unlearned can scarcely mistake them—Murillo being all softness, while Velazquez is all sparkle and vivacity.[2]

---

[1] Cunningham's "Life of Wilkie," II., pp. 484-487, Journal.
[2] Cunningham's "Life of Wilkie," p. 472. Letter to Sir Thos. Lawrence.

IX.

THE SCHOOL OF MADRID.

In the earlier Spanish painters there is little apparent love of nature; in art as in literature, to the early painter the world of nature is less attractive than the world of human life. Living man rather than landscape is his theme. In later times, when society grows older and more commonplace, the tendency is to retire in weariness and to seek communion with the quiet of nature. Æschylus has suggested here a fruitful thought, when in "Prometheus," the sad, desolate god, bound to the rock, first breaks the silence with his sublime apostrophe to the sea and the powers of living nature, as if he would find there his only remaining source of sympathy. The artist of our age, desolate and chained to the rock of self-consuming torture, pours out his griefs before the shrine of external nature.

There was no knowledge of nature in the early Spanish followers of Italian traditions. But a nobler awakening of Spanish genius was at hand. The art of the great masters was objective,—employed in the simple, lifelike portraiture of nature, of human character, their landscapes were real. It is true that man, in the great age of Spanish art, was the centre of artistic life; and natural description was only the accessory. But nowhere do we find more magnificent pictures of nature than in Velazquez ; and even Murillo and Cano are accurate in painting their landscape, even if it be only a background to their figures.

At this time appears Francisco Collantes, the great Spanish landscape-painter. Born in 1599, Collantes early entered the studio of Vicente Carducho. Like most young painters of his day, while educated in the Italian traditions, he yet breathed in with the air about him a love of the real. His early works bear the mark of Carducho's teaching ; but he soon showed an independent bent. His landscapes—" The Burning Bush," "a silvan scene full of massy foliage and mellow sunshine," now at the Louvre ; and several pictures in the Academy of San Fernando and in the Prado; of the latter, especially " a landscape with trees and a brawling brook,"—compare favourably, in their intensity of colour, their vigorous expression, and powerful effects, with the best landscapes of the Venetian and Bolognese schools.

There exist but few works of Collantes. " Of these, Ezekiel in the valley of bones, formerly at Buenretiro, is the most striking. The 'exceedingly great army' of skeletons are bestirring and refreshing themselves as beheld in that mysterious vision; the brown mountain background is well painted, and the figure of the Seer, in blue drapery, is worthy of Salvator Rosa." [1]

---

[1] Stirling-Maxwell, p. 706.

Collantes painted *bodegones* with much skill, and Cean Bermudez praises his spirited sketches in red ink. He died at Madrid in 1656.

Fray Juan Rizi, son of Antonio Rizi, was born at Madrid in 1595. He was a pupil of Juan Bautista Mayno. In 1626 he entered the Convent of Monserrat; during many years his religious duties alienated him from his art; but in 1653 he executed a remarkable series for the Convent of San Millan de Cogolla y Yuso. Over the high altar and in the cloisters were scenes from the life of the saint; and on the grand stairway was a magnificent painting of the "Children of the Order of St. Benedict"; a noble composition, brilliant in colour, and remarkable for its skilful arrangement of the group and the varied expression of the faces. In the Convent of San Juan Bautista, at Burgos, are several fine works of Rizi—a "Holy Family," scenes from the "Life of the Virgin," "Baptism of Christ," and the "Beheading of John the Baptist." Rizi's best work was executed for the Convent of San Martin, at Madrid, to which series belong the "Pilgrims of Emmaus," and several scenes from the life of St. Benedict. Two of these—St. Benedict blessing a loaf of bread presented him by a lay-brother, and St. Benedict with the abbot's cross—are now in the *Museo Nacional*, at Madrid. One of his noblest compositions is now in the Academy of San Fernando—"St. Benedict Celebrating Mass." It is a powerful painting, rich in colour, and effective in design. His "St. Francis Receiving the

Stigmata," in the Prado, is also fine. His work lacks careful finish; but the design is telling, the composition free and simple. Later in life Rizi visited Italy and continued his work in the retreat of Monte Cassino, where he died in 1675.

Francisco Rizi was born at Madrid in 1608. He was a pupil of Vicente Carducho. "Seldom was a youth," says Cean Bermudez, "more plentifully endowed with dispositions and talents for painting. There was no object, figure, or attitude that Rizi could not draw, as it were, off-hand; and the effect of this habit of off-hand drawing was that he never drew any thing with perfect accuracy. He lived in an age and at a court where the arts of improvisation were highly valued and applauded; he secured a considerable share of contemporary fame at the least possible cost, and he thought as little of posterity as posterity has thought of him." [1]

Rizi was prolific in grand religious compositions, in fresco, in scenic decoration, in historic subjects, in portrait, and indeed in almost every style of painting.

In 1653 he painted for the sacristy of the Cathedral of Toledo a "Dedication of the Cathedral"; he was then appointed painter to the chapter; and in 1665 was associated with Carreño in the frescoes of the Chapel *del Ochavo*. In 1656 Philip IV. made Rizi painter in ordinary. He decorated at that time the Buenretiro, but in a style so extravagant and fantastic, and in such bad

---

[1] Stirling-Maxwell, p. 696.

taste, that Cean Bermudez says he did more than any one else to hasten the spread of meretricious art throughout Spain. In the Prado are two works of Francisco Rizi; one represents an *auto-da-fe* in the reign of Charles II. It is a very curious historical composition, giving the Plaza Mayor, with the old buildings of the Inquisition, and the spot where heretics were solemnly burned in those good old days, and portraits of the king and courtiers, with the ecclesiastical dignitaries of the time. The other painting is a portrait of an unknown knight of Calatrava, a noble picture, with rich, harmonious colour, and broad, free handling. Rizi was a rapid painter, and he has left numerous paintings scattered among the churches of Madrid.

Francisco Rizi died at the Escorial in 1685. Of his scholars were Claudio Coello, Isidoro Arredondo, Gonzalo de la Vega, Juan Antonio Escalante, and Josef Antolinez.

Juan Bautista Martinez del Mazo was born at Madrid. He early entered the studio of Velazquez, where he worked untiringly, copying his master, Titian, Tintoretto, and Paul Veronese. Mazo married a daughter of Velazquez, and in his art followed closely in his master's footsteps. His most important work was in landscape and hunting pieces. There is now in the Prado a fine picture of Zaragoza executed by Mazo for the king, Philip IV. The view is taken from the banks of the Ebro; on the farther bank rise the turrets and walls of the distant city;

in the foreground is a fine group of figures, executed by Velazquez. " For richness and brilliancy of effect it is equal to the best of Canaletto's views of Dresden, which it much resembles in style." [1]

Mazo was an admirable portrait-painter; his pictures resemble very closely those of Velazquez,—the same rich colour and fine treatment; but they are heavier, they lack the sparkle and vivacity of Velazquez. His reputation as a portrait-painter was won by his portrait of Queen Mariana, " which he exhibited at the gate of Guadalajara, and which attracted much attention, because it was one of the first pictures executed of the young sovereign at Madrid." [2]

In the Prado are a fine full-length portrait of an unknown captain, of the time of Philip IV., and ten landscapes. Of these, after the view of Zaragoza, a seaport and a river view are the most noteworthy.

At the death of Velazquez, Mazo was made painter in ordinary, which post he occupied under Charles II. also. He died in 1687.

Juan de Pareja, the mulatto slave of Velazquez, was born at Seville in 1606. He went to Madrid with Velazquez in 1623, and was employed by him in the menial work of grinding colours, cleaning brushes, and preparing palettes. He was early tempted to try handling the brush, and in his leisure moments he copied his master's works " with the eagerness of a lover and the secrecy of

---

[1] Stirling-Maxwell, p. 712.
[2] Stirling-Maxwell, p. 711.

a conspirator." He accompanied his master to Italy, and while there sought to improve in his art; "but his nature was so reserved, and his candle so jealously concealed under its bushel, that he had returned from his second visit to Rome, and had reached the mature age of forty-five, before his master became aware that he could use the brushes which he washed.

"When at last he determined on laying aside his mask, he contrived that it should be removed by the hand of the king. Finishing a small picture with peculiar care, he deposited it in his master's studio, with its face turned to the wall. A picture so placed arouses curiosity, and is perhaps more certain to attract the eye of the loitering visitor than if it were hung up for the purpose of being seen. When Philip IV. visited Velazquez he never failed to cause the daub or the masterpiece, that happened to occupy such a position, to be paraded for his inspection. He therefore fell at once into the trap, and, being pleased with the work, asked for the author. Pareja, who took care to be at the royal elbow, immediately fell on his knees, owning his guilt and praying for his Majesty's protection. The good-natured king, turning to Velazquez, said: 'You see that a painter like this ought not to remain a slave.' Pareja, kissing the royal hand, rose from the ground a free man: his master gave him a formal deed of manumission, and received the colour-grinder as a scholar." [1] Pareja remained in his master's service; still

---

Stirling-Maxwell, II., pp. 708, 709.

he could now give himself up to his art. It is to this time, undoubtedly, that his larger paintings belong, as the " Calling of St. Matthew," now in the Prado. " It is well composed, and executed with a close and successful imitation of the colouring and handling of Velazquez. Our Lord and his disciples wear the flowing Jewish gaberdine, the collectors of customs, doublets and flapped hats, and are booted and spurred like Spanish cavaliers. The dusky face to the extreme right of the picture is a portrait of the painter ; and the rich Turkey carpet which covers the table, and the jewellery thereon displayed, are finished with Dutch minuteness." [1] In the *Museo Nacional* are three paintings by Pareja: the " Baptism of Christ," executed for the Convent of la Trinidad, at Toledo ; the " Presentation of Christ in the Temple," and a Battle Piece. These are the only works of Pareja now in Spain. But it is as a portrait-painter that Pareja merits especial notice. It is probable that many of his portraits are attributed to Mazo and others of the school of Velazquez, and it is sometimes difficult to distinguish them. In the Hermitage is a fine portrait of a capuchin provincial,—a careful, life-like figure in dark monastic robes, holding a book in his hand ; it is a work of great merit.

Pareja remained in the service of Velazquez and of his daughter, the wife of Mazo, until his death in 1670.

Don Juan Carreño de Miranda was born at Aviles in the Asturias in 1614. In 1623 he came with his father

---

[1] Stirling-Maxwell, p. 710.

to Madrid, where he was placed in the studio of Pedro
de las Cuevas, an old Madrid painter, and the master of
Antonio Pereda, Jusepe Leonardo, Francisco Camilo,
etc.   Pedro de las Cuevas was a painter in the Florentine
manner, and with him, says Bermudez, Carreño learned
to draw.   He studied colour later with Bartolomé
Roman.

In 1634 Carreño executed several works for the
cloisters of the college of Doña Maria of Aragon and
for the Church *del Rosario*, and from that time forward
his works are numerous and important.

In 1650 he established a school of painting at Madrid,
where among other pupils we find Mateo Cerezo.

In 1653 he began his great frescoes for the churches of
Madrid ; and at about the same time he was associated
with Francisco Rizi in certain works for the Cathedral of
Toledo.

In 1659 Carreño was made painter to the king by
Philip IV., and in 1671 the young Charles II. appointed
him painter in ordinary and deputy-*Aposentador*.

, Carreño was a great favourite with the young king,
whose feeble face figures again and again on the painter's canvas.   Charles loved him extraordinarily, says Bermudez—*le amaba extraordinariamente,*—and many are the
anecdotes Palomino relates of the distinguished artist.
On one occasion, while sitting for his portrait, the king
asked Carreño of what order he was.   " Of none,"
answered the painter; " I have but the honour of serving

your majesty." The cross of Santiago was then sent to him ; but when his friends told him that being nobly born he needed no such distinction, and that he should accept it as an honour paid to his art, he exclaimed: "*La pintura no necesita honores, ella puede darlos a todo el mundo.*" (Painting needs no honours, but can give them to all the world.) In spite of his prominent position and the favours showered on him by the king, Carreño was simple and unspoiled. He was a man of easy temper, and seldom took offense. Palomino tells us that he was with him one day at the house of Don Pedro de Arce, when the conversation turned on a copy of Titian's St. Margaret, which hung in the room. It was condemned by all, and the unknown painter severely criticised. "It at least shews," said Carreño, "that a man need not despair of improving in art, for I myself painted it when I was a beginner."

At the death of Velazquez Carreño took the place of court painter, and his portraits are not unworthy to hang on the same walls with the master's works. Much of the free touch and splendid colour of Velazquez are his ; but they are sometimes tempered by an harmonious softness which recalls Van Dyck. No other painter so closely approaches the manner of Velazquez. In the Prado is a portrait of Francisco Bazan, a dwarf and buffoon, which for a long time was attributed to Velazquez. Carreño pourtrayed the different members of the royal family and the grandees. Six fine examples of his work as a portrait-painter are in the Prado. One of the finest of these represents the Russian ambassador, Pedro Iwanowiz Potemkin, a full-length figure in a red robe, which recalls Titian.

Carreño died in 1685.

Chief among Carreño's pupils was Mateo Cerezo, born at Burgos in 1635. Cerezo at first studied with his father, and in 1650 he entered the studio of Carreño at Madrid. He learned rapidly, and at twenty-three was known as a painter of great promise. He was soon after this associated with Herrera el Mozo in his work at Our Lady of Atocha. In 1668 he executed one of his finest works, the "Magdalen," now at Vienna. In the museums of Berlin and the Hague are replicas of this picture. Cerezo, unlike many Spanish painters, while he painted only religious subjects, yet chose no scenes of dramatic horror, but rather pourtrayed the Madonna and the Magdalen. He excelled, above all, in pictures of the Conception. His colour is soft and harmonious; his design pure and delicate. His paintings are found in every country, and are often attributed to Murillo. One of his finest works, the Supper at Emmaus, was executed for the refectory of the *Recolitos* shortly before his death, which occurred in 1685.

Claudio Coello was born at Madrid, of Portuguese parents, in 1621. He studied under Francisco Rizi, who early marked his great talent. While yet in Rizi's studio he executed several altar-pieces for the Monastery

of San Placido, and for the churches of San Andres and
Santa Cruz. The latter so pleased Rizi that he offered
to have them pass as his own work, that the young artist
might be paid for his labour.

Coello studied awhile with Carreño, desiring instruction in colour, and by that painter was admitted to the
royal galleries, where he copied the masterpieces of
Titian, Rubens, and Van Dyck. He next associated
himself with Ximenez Donoso, who had just returned
from Rome, whence he brought a most meretricious
style. They were employed together in work in Santa
Cruz, in the Cathedral of Toledo, in the churches of San
Isidro el Real, La Trinidad, and San Basilio, and in the
Alcazar. They also designed the decorations for the
triumphal arches at the entry of Queen Maria Luisa into
Madrid; the great arch of the Prado, representing the
kingdoms of Spain offering flowers, fruits, and jewels
to the young queen has been engraved. Coello also
designed a series of the "Labours of Hercules," which
was painted by Francisco de Solis.

In 1683 Coello executed in fresco the cupola of the
Collegiate Church of the Augustins at Zaragoza; in the
following year he was made painter to the king, and two
years later painter in ordinary in the place of Herrera el
Mozo. He succeeded also to the position of Carreño,
and at the death of Francisco Rizi he was called to complete the altar-piece in the great sacristy of the Escorial.
There was kept here a most precious relic, the *Santa*

Forma, a sacramental wafer, which, outraged by the Zwinglians, had been the subject of a great miracle at Gorcum in Holland.   Charles II., wishing to dedicate a new altar to the *Santa Forma*, chose Rizi for the task, and at his death Coello was called on to complete the *retablo*.   Throwing aside Rizi's design, Coello, after three years' labour, succeeded in achieving a great success.   It was a difficult task he had undertaken,   " IIis canvas was six yards high by only three wide, and his subject nothing more nor less than Charles II. and his court receiving the sacerdotal benediction at the dedication of the altar. From these unpromising materials he produced a work of great power and splendour, and one of the most interesting pictures which has been spared to the desolate Escorial.   The king and his courtiers are represented kneeling before the altar adoring the holy Host, which is held up by the officiating prior.   Around that dignitary are grouped his assistant priests ; in the distance are seen the Jeronymite friars drawn up in processional order,   the students of the college and the boys of the choir, chaunting under the orders of the chapel-master, while above hover three allegorical figures representing Religion, Piety, and the house of Austria, in contemplation of the splendid scene.   The picture contains, it is said, no less than fifty portraits, to most of which, unfortunately, there now exists no key.   The king himself, gazing at the mysterious relique with a face of foolish awe, is evidently pourtrayed to the very life.   Near him kneel the Duke of

Medina-celi, a prime-minister almost as weak as his master; his rival, the Duke of Pastrana, grand-huntsman; the
Count of Baños, master of the horse; and the Marquess
of la Puebla, gentleman of the chamber. The astute-
looking prior is said to be Francisco de los Santos, the
historian of the Escorial. Nothing can be more brilliant
and masterly than the execution of the rich robes of the
churchmen, and the more sober suits of the laity.
* * * The portable organ of Charles V., the crucifix,
the candlesticks, and the other accessories of the ceremo-
nial are all painted with great care." [1] Coello was now at
the zenith of his power; he was called on to pourtray the
Dowager Queen Mariana, the Queen Mariana, Charles'
second wife, and all the grandees. He had also charge of
restoring the pictures in the royal gallery.

In 1691 he was made painter to the Toledan Chapter,
a title that had been conferred on no one since the death
of Rizi. In the midst of his fame and glory the king
called Luca Giordano to Madrid, to be employed at the
Escorial. He arrived in May, 1692, and in less than a
year Coello died of a broken heart—of a disease which, if
not brought on, was at least fostered, by his mortification
at seeing a stranger placed above the foremost painter of
Spain.

Before Giordano's arrival, a friend said to him: " Giordano will teach you how to grow rich." "Yes," exclaimed Coello, "and also how to rid us of our scruples

---

[1] Stirling-Maxwell, III., pp. 1014, 1015, 1016.

and to excuse our faults." A painter of genius, an anxious and careful draughtsman, a bold colourist, Coello was a marked contrast to Luca *fa presto.* He sought to combine Cano's graceful design, Murillo's colour, and Velazquez's magic effect; and he failed as the Caracci failed. But, withal, Coello was a great painter, the last of his race in Spain. Had he lived in the day of Philip II., says Cean Bermudez, he had been one of our best painters. But his day befell in the declining time of Spanish art.

X.

CONTEMPORARIES AND FOLLOWERS OF MURILLO.

WE know little of the character of Juan de Valdes Leal save from the scenes in which he appears as the jealous rival of Murillo or other painters: but in these we behold the man sketched in the boldest lines. He had not a genuine and mastering love of art; he was rather an egotist, envious of all other talent than his own.

Born at Cordova in 1630, Valdes Leal studied awhile with Antonio del Castillo. He came early to Seville, where he found Murillo in the zenith of his glory. When the Academy was opened in 1660 he was made *mayor domo*, an office which he filled during several months; but his jealous disposition made him relinquish it. Three years later he was chosen president; but in 1666 his arrogant temper had so embroiled him with the other members that he gave up all connection with the association. A story related by Palomino shews his narrow, envious spirit. While yet president, he was asked by an Italian painter, a stranger in Seville, permission to draw in the Academy. Valdes denied the request; but it was granted by the patrons of the Academy. On his first appearance the Italian went boldly to work, covering a sheet of white

paper with charcoal, and dashing off a rapid sketch with
marvellous dexterity, by rubbing out the high lights and
half tones with a bit of bread ; he finished two or three
figures in the evening.   Valdes, the boldest draughtsman
in the Association, could not bear the stranger's success ;
and refused him further entrance to the Academy.   Vexed
by this treatment, the Italian painter bought two pieces
of canvas and painted on them a " Crucifixion," and the
figure of a " St. Sebastian," executed with great skill ;
these found immediate purchasers when offered for sale
on the cathedral steps.   Irritated by the praise showered
on the painter, and the blame attributed to himself,
Valdes threatened the stranger's life, who fled from the
city.   This is but one of many incidents in which Valdes
proved himself a worthy countryman of the overbearing
Spagnoletto.

But with all his arrogance, Valdes is one of the great
masters of the school of Seville.   With a bold, vigorous
touch resembling that of Herrera, and a grand conception,
but often marred by hasty execution, he sacrificed much
to scenic effect.   His colour is powerful and striking, but
he lacks harmony and grace.   A sombre, passionate
nature, he sought rather to astonish than to charm.

In the Caridad are two most characteristic works of
Valdes.   " They still occupy their original place, on either
side of the great door of the church, beneath the choir of
the gallery.   One represents a table heaped with tiaras,
crowns, badges of knighthood, and other gewgaws of state,

with a taper beside them, which Death, carrying a coffin under one arm, extinguishes with the bony fingers of the other hand. Round the flame of the taper are the words IN ICTU OCULI. On the floor there is an open coffin, with its velvet and ornaments tattered and broken, and revealing a crowned and grinning corpse within. The companion piece represents a hand holding a pair of scales, in which the sins of the world, in the form of bats, peacocks, serpents, and other symbolical creatures are weighed against the nails, reed, and the rest of the emblems of the cross and passion of Our Lord, and found wanting. Over the sinful scale is written NIMAS, over the other NIMENOS. The floor is strewed with books and mathematical instruments. It was to the first of these pictures that Murillo paid the pleasant but equivocal compliment 'that it was so forcibly painted that it was necessary to hold one's nose when looking at it.' "[1]

Valdes left numerous works in Cordova and Seville. In the cathedral of the latter city is a powerful "Scourging of Christ," a noble "St. Ildefonso Receiving the *Casulla*," and in the *Museo* are several fine examples of his masculine art. The Prado contains two pictures only of Valdes: the "Presentation of the Virgin," and the "Emperor Constantine at Prayer."

The death of Murillo in 1682 left Valdes the first and strongest painter of Seville. His work was so arduous in these later years that in much of it he was assisted by his

---

[1] Stirling-Maxwell, pp. 1098, 1099.

son Lucas. While painting, in 1690, a series of pictures for the Church of *los Venerables*, he was struck with paralysis and died in the following year.

Valdes Leal left several pupils of note, among whom were his son Lucas de Valdes, Matias de Arteaga, Ignacio de Leon, Antonio Palomino, Cristobal de Leon, Pedro de Uceda, and Clemente de Torres. His daughters, Maria and Luisa de Valdes, were admirable portrait-painters, excelling above all in miniature.

Ignacio Iriarte was born in 1620, at Azcoitia. In 1642 he entered the studio of Herrera *el Viejo*, with whom he made an especial study of colour. Iriarte was an intimate friend of Murillo; during several years they were associated in their work, Iriarte making the backgrounds to Murillo's figures. They could not, however, agree as to which should first paint his portion, so that Murillo learned to put in his own landscape. Iriarte's landscapes are of the conventional order—artificial and ornate—rather the work of a skilled decorator than of a landscape-painter. His colour is soft and harmonious; his execution admirable; he seems to have taken Murillo as his model. His paintings are very rare. In the Prado there are three of his best landscapes. "In the National Museum there is also a pleasing work, a cataract dashing amongst brown crags and old trees, and a range of blue mountains in the distance."[1]

Iriarte was secretary for nine years in the Academy of Design, founded at Seville in 1660. He died in 1685.

---

[1] Stirling-Maxwell, p. 934.

Pedro de Moya was born at Seville in 1610. He entered early the studio of Juan del Castillo. But Castillo's teaching did not satisfy the young painter. He needed larger and freer influences. Too poor to travel, he enlisted as a common soldier, thus reaching the Low Countries, where he passed each leisure moment in the museums and churches, copying the great Flemish masters. The paintings of Van Dyck above all others attracted him. An enthusiast in his art, he left the army and hastened to England. Van Dyck received him with open arms; and brought him into his studio. The master's untimely death, before six months had passed, cast Moya again adrift. He gathered together his sketches and returned to Seville; and there he implanted a knowledge and love for Van Dyck which bore rapid fruit among the young Sevillian painters. We already know its influence on the young Murillo.

After passing a short time in Seville, Moya established himself at Granada, and devoted himself to work in the churches and convents of the neighboring country. In 1651 Alonso Cano came to Granada, and these two artists founded the small but important school of Granada. Its most prominent names are those of Juan de Sevilla, Anastasio Bocanegra, Niño de Guevara, Sebastian Gomez, and Geronimo de Cieza. The noble, chaste style of Cano, with its classic severity, united to the wealth of Flemish colour of Moya, created a worthy and original manner in their followers.

But few traces of Moya's work remain. In the Cathedral of Granada one of his altar-pieces represents the Virgin and Child appearing to a kneeling bishop, and in the Prado is a fine series of six pictures from the history of Joseph. Moya was an able painter, possessing a free touch, yet careful execution, a rich soft colour and harmonious outlines; but his paintings recall now Van Dyck, now Rubens, now Murillo, and have little originality of style. Moya died at Granada in 1666.

Juan de Sevilla Romero y Escalante was born at Granada in 1637. He studied at first under a third-rate artist, Andres Alonso Argüelle, but soon entered the studio of Pedro de Moya. At Moya's death, in 1666, Sevilla devoted some time to copying the works of Rubens, and learned the secret of the Flemish colour. He executed four paintings for the Cathedral at Granada; two of which, the most important, represent the martyrdom of St. Cecilia, and St. Basilio giving the rules of his order to St. Benedict. These pictures possess a chaste, elegant design, and a wealth of colour that recalls Van Dyck. Sevilla executed several paintings for the *Franciscanos*, the *Carmelitas*, and the *Augustinos;* and for the refectory of the Jesuit College he painted a noble "Last Supper." There is a fine picture of St. Augustine, the Virgin, and the Infant Christ now in the Museum at Granada. " His colouring was rich and forcible, and had he been disposed to communicate his knowledge, he might have done somewhat toward staying the decline of painting at Granada."

He received no scholars in his studio; his biographers give as reason his jealousy of his beautiful wife Teresa de Rueda. Sevilla died in 1695.

Pedro Anastasio Bocanegra was also a native of Granada and a pupil of Alonso Cano. He joined to his master's teaching a careful study of Moya's works and thus acquired that pleasing union of classic grace and rich Flemish colour which we find in the school of Granada. He seems to have been a man of inordinate conceit. He was involved in endless rivalries with his fellow painters. In Madrid he gained great praise by some work executed for the king; and at this time he was made painter-to-the-king. But his vain boasts made him the laughing-stock of the city and finally drove him thence. In his old age he entered into competition with Teodoro Ardemans. The proposed trial of skill was that each artist should, in a given time, paint the other's portrait. Ardemans, the first to begin, seized his palette and brush, and in less than an hour, had made a striking sketch of his rival. Bocanegra, disheartened at the young painter's triumph, put off his sketch until the morrow, and then failed utterly in his first attempt. Rage and mortification caused his death a few days later. But however contemptible the man,—the artist left many noble works in his native city. In the cathedral are some of the finest. Cean Bermudez mentions worth special praise a *retablo*, representing " San Pedro Nolasco finding the choir of his convent occupied by the Virgin and company of angels ";

also a " Crucifixion," which he thinks might pass for the work of Van Dyck.

Miguel Geronimo de Cieza, also of Granada, was one of the best of the school of Cano. In the Hermitage of San Miguel is a " Madonna and Child," and " Christ with the Woman at the Well of Samaria," and in the Church of San Pedro and the Convent of Los Angelos are several fine works of Cieza.

Cieza's two sons, Josef and Vicente, studied with their father. They settled in Madrid, where they were both successful in their profession. Vicente returned in 1701 to Granada, where he died soon afterward. His pictures there are often mistaken for his father's work.

We come now to the pupils and imitators of Murillo. Sebastian Gomez, *el Mulato di Murillo*, was, like Pareja, employed in the menial work of his master's studio. Endowed with great natural talent, and with ample opportunity to study his art in secret, he acquired a skill equalled by few of Murillo's pupils. When the time was ripe for the discovery of his secret, he made himself known by finishing a head of the Virgin, a sketch which lay on his master's easel. Delighted with the discovery, Murillo exclaimed : " I am indeed fortunate, Sebastian, for I have created not only pictures but a painter." Gomez died at Seville in 1682, the same year as his master. His works have a rich, harmonious colour, but are deficient in accuracy of drawing. He painted for the *Mercenarios Descalzos* a "Virgin and Child," and a " Christ at the

Column," with St. Peter kneeling at his feet, and for the *Capuchinos*, "St. Joseph and Sta. Anna"; these pictures exist no longer. In the *Musco* is a beautiful "Conception" which recalls Murillo most strongly, and in the *Contaduria* of the cathedral is a fine "Holy Family."

Pedro Nuñez de Villavicencio was born at Seville, in 1635. He was of a noble Andalusian family and a knight of the order of St. John of Jerusalem. He was a pupil of Murillo, who recognized his unusual talent. Obliged by the duties of his order to leave Seville and repair to Malta, he studied there awhile under Matias Preti, called Il Calabrese. On his return to Seville he became a member of the Academy and renewed his friendship with Murillo. After the master's death he went to Madrid, where he painted for Charles II. a group, now in the Prado, "representing two boys wrangling over the dice, which they are throwing upon an old cloak, spread on the ground. Behind them there is another youngster, who slyly abstracts a portion of the copper stakes, and a girl taking care of a child; and in the background there is a landscape with figures."[1]

It is in the style of Murillo, and a very life-like work. Villavicencio presented to the Count of Monterey a picture in the same style. For the *Carmelitas* at Madrid he executed several scenes in the life of the Virgin. He was an admirable portrait-painter: one of his best portraits was

---

[1] Stirling-Maxwell, p. 1105.

that of the Archbishop Ambrosio Spinola of Seville, which was engraved.   Villavicencio died at Seville in 1700.

Francisco Meneses Osorio was another of Murillo's pupils, and a most happy imitator of his great master. He has much of the charm of Murillo's style, and of his rich, soft colouring. He accompanied Murillo to Cadiz in 1680; and after Murillo's fall from the scaffolding, he completed the picture of the " Marriage of St, Catharine." He settled at Seville, where he was assisted in much of his work by Juan Garzon, another pupil of Murillo, who died in 1700.   In the Church of San Martin, at Seville, is a fine picture of the " Prophet Elijah in the Desert Comforted by an Angel"; and in the hospital at Cadiz are four of his works: one, a " Guardian Angel Leading a Little Child," recalls Murillo's picture on the same subject, at Seville.   It is supposed that Meneses executed the large work in the Merced at Cadiz, representing San Cayetano opening his arms to the Child Jesus; it is painted from a sketch by Murillo.

Alonso Miguel de Tobar, the best of the copyists of Murillo, was born at Higuera in 1678. He studied at Seville under a third-rate painter, Juan Antonio Faxardo. Dissatisfied with Faxardo's instruction, Tobar turned toward Murillo, and devoted himself to the study of his works.   He studied them until he had thoroughly learned the master's style, and made copies which were often mistaken for original works.   " Tobar is perhaps the artist whose counterfeits most rarely suffer detection.   In

colouring he imitates Murillo closely and happily; he
selects faces of the same expression, and draperies of the
same shades; and in his more elaborate efforts he falls
short of his model in little except his inimitable round-
ness of forms and absence of outline.

"The picture in the chapel of Our Lady of Consolation,
in the Cathedral of Seville, is generally esteemed his
masterpiece, and certainly is a composition of great
merit. It represents the Virgin, in blue and white drapery,
with the Infant Saviour in her lap, and adored by saints;
and it bears the painter's signature, 'Dn. Alonso Miguel
Tobar, ffamiliar del So. Officio ffet Ao. 1720.' "[1]

Esteban Marquez, a native of Estramadura, was a pupil
of his uncle Fernando Marquez Joya of the school of
Murillo. At Joya's death, Marquez was employed
awhile in painting for the weekly *Feria* the rough pictures
that were sent in great numbers to America. But he
lacked the rapid pencil and free, bold touch needed for
such work; discouraged he returned to his native village,
only to be drawn back to Seville by his overpowering love
of art, to which he devoted himself with renewed vigour.
He soon excelled as an imitator and copyist of Murillo.
He equals Meneses Osorio and Tobar in his copies of
the master, and is, doubtless, the author of many works
attributed to Murillo. In the Hospital del Sangre is
a fine series, representing "Christ, the Virgin, and the
twelve apostles"; and in the Museum is a charming

[1] Stirling-Maxwell, p. 1305.

" St. Joseph with the Infant Christ." For the *Trinitarios Descalzos* he painted a fine Ascension ; a noble composition treated in a broad, free manner, and containing several fine heads.

Marquez died at Seville in 1720.

Francisco Antolinez y Sarabia was born at Seville in 1644. Although educated for the Bar he had great love of art and studied for some time with Murillo ; he became, too, a member of the Academy of Design. In 1672 he joined his uncle, the painter Josef Antolinez, at Madrid, where, on the latter's death in 1676, he began the practice of law. He supported himself, however, by his pencil, although he continued in what he fancied a more dignified profession. At his wife's death he determined to take orders, and had just returned to Madrid for that purpose when he died in 1700. " He was " says Palomino, " in spite of his strange temper and unsettled habits, a man of large erudition and great powers of memory, and had an apposite quotation on his tongue for every incident or subject that could occur."

Antolinez was an able draughtsman and a graceful, pleasing colourist. In the *Museo Nacional* at Madrid are five pictures executed for the Church of San Felipe. The subjects are the " Purification of the Virgin "; " Adoration "; " Flight into Egypt "; " Annunciation," and " Marriage of the Virgin." In the Cathedral of Seville there is a fine " Nativity."

Palomino says that he saw a small picture by Antolinez,

which represented the Virgin in Egypt assisted by some pious women in washing the clothing of the Infant Saviour. He mistook it for a work of Murillo, and valued it at a hundred pesos.

Antolinez painted chiefly landscapes; his pictures are generally small. He excelled, too, in portraits and miniatures.

Bernardo Geronimo de Llorente was born at Seville in 1685. He studied under Cristobal Lopez, and devoted himself to the imitation of Murillo. An able painter, he was recognized everywhere as such; but his morbid habit and gloomy disposition made him refuse all honours, even that of painter-to-the-king. He was, however, elected member of the Academy of San Fernando. He is known as *el pintor de las Pastoras*, from his charming representations of the Virgin as a shepherdess. His most important work, in this subject, was for many years attributed to Tobar, but has been restored to Llorente in the revised catalogue. " It represents our Lady in a pastoral dress, seated beneath a tree and feeding lambs on roses. The head of the Blessed Virgin, covered with dark-blue drapery, and with the ' loose train of her amber-dropping hair,' in conception is worthy of Alonso Cano, and the details of the picture, the spreading tree, the hovering cherubs, the rose-fed lambs, and the distant landscape, in which is seen a strayed sheep delivered by an angel from the jaws of a dragon, are finished with elaborate care. This graceful religious fancy was first put forward,

says Cean Bermudez, early in the eighteenth century by
Fray Isidoro, a Capuchin of Seville. Our Lord, in likening
himself to a vine, had compared the Eternal Father to a
husbandman.   Hence, perhaps, the idea of representing
the Virgin Mother of him who described himself as the
good shepherd, in the guise of a shepherdess.   But whatever its origin, the conceit became very popular, and under
the especial patronage of the Franciscan order, spread over
all Spain, and bade fair to supplant the Immaculate Conception itself in the affections of the faithful." [1]

Cean Bermudez mentions several works of Llorente,
which have all disappeared.   He was an able painter,
though his touch is heavy, and he lacks the soft,
harmonious colour, the accurate drawing, and the clearly
defined shadows of Murillo ; he used much bitumen in
his colours, which has blackened and in some cases utterly
ruined much of his work.

Llorente died at Seville in 1757.

We come now to a host of imitators and copyists of
Murillo.   Andres Perez, Josef de Rubira, Alonso de
Escobar, Juan Simon Gutierrez, Joaquin Josef Cano,
Josef Lopez, Matio Gonzalo, Clemente de Torres are the
foremost.   If we analyze their painting it is rather its
form than its artistic thought that attracts us.   They
weave around a commonplace sentiment their many-
tinted imagery ; but they remind us of the mosaic-
workers of modern Italy, who can put together, now that

---

[1] Stirling-Maxwell, pp. 1305, 1306.

the creator of a Transfiguration is gone, the most perfect copies of it in bits of coloured glass.

They have all one grand fault.   It is that from first to last they have sacrificed art to effect.   They are skilful colourists; but they are void of creative power.   Imitation is the characteristic of them all.   They reproduce Murillo.   There is a style of handling by which a third-rate artist can give us a picture very like the master; not indeed a marvel of art, but its most obvious strokes. And as we gaze at the canvas we can almost swear it is Murillo's work; the same soft, harmonious colour, the same gracious sentiment.   Their canvases are the ornaments of the master without his power, a confection of sugared trifles.   Solomon said: "Hast thou found honey?   Eat so much as is sufficient for thee, lest thou be cloyed therewith."   His injunction applies to all of these surfeiting copyists.

XI.

THE DECLINE OF SPANISH ART.

WE have seen the earliest revelation of a pure art in Morales and Juanes, the powerful national type in Roelas and Zurbaran, the glory of Velazquez and Murillo. But we are now to study the time of its decay.

Spain had just passed through a splendid period of genius. After the day of Velazquez, Murillo, and their immediate followers, it seemed as if the creative power of the Spanish mind had passed away, and art was buried in their grave. With the painters who followed them, there came an epoch of imitation and affectation. There was never a time when more was produced, when the pencil was more active. But it is impossible to look at the pictures of that day without feeling that there has never been, at any time, a worse type of a dead art, with all the vices that it engenders, than is found in the mannerists of that day. Luca Giordano is the type of that perverted art; to him Spanish painting had declined in the long lineage of sacred names,—Morales, Navarrete, Roelas, Zurbaran, Velazquez. Giordano did not ask whether their art might still be perfected. He put on the gewgaws of rank, entered in vain pride the Escorial, faced the visions of a Navarrete, and believed himself greater than Velazquez. He represents the backward current which swept Spanish art from nature to a dead *fare da se.* His rapid pencil, which won for him the name of *Luca fa presto,* his extraordinary facility in every style, fostered the worst vices of the Spanish painters. They had insufficiently studied the nude : and, in consequence, a looseness and inaccuracy of drawing had always characterized Spanish art. From this abyss Velazquez and Murillo had been rescued only by their close studies direct from nature. Giordano was a man of talent and original power, which made his influence more dangerous. " His great ' Battle of St. Quintin' on the Staircase of the Escorial, is a striking work—the more so, perhaps, because its tumult and confusion contrast singularly enough with the quiet grey aspect of the granite frame-work in which it is set, and with the noiseless solemnity of the building it adorns." [1]

Giordano left Spain in 1702, after passing ten years in rapid work which has filled galleries, churches, palaces, and above all, the Escorial, with his paintings. He returned to Naples, where he died in 1705. His art was a mass of bric-a-brac, and this character is the mark of the mind that produced it. It was a day of bric-a-brac, incapable of that completeness of thought which can create *Las Lanzas* or *Las Hilanderas,* or any thing, save fitful attempts at originality. There were all schools and types of pretension. The painters sought far and wide for some striking

---

[1] Head, p. 206.

fancy which should smite and astonish the eye; and, like most imitators, they were often tempted to affect novelties purely for the sake of surprise.

The character of true art is truth to the thought, that style where the artistic ideas are one with the expression, where the colours only seem to rise and overflow because they are borne along by the inspiration : but in the artists of this time there was no inspiration.

It is the writer not the artist who attracts us in Palomino. Acisclo Antonio Palomino y Velasco was born at Bujalance, in 1653. He pursued his classical studies at Cordova, where, in 1672, he met Valdes Leal, by whose advice the young student devoted himself to art. In 1675 Juan de Alfaro visited Cordova, and, much struck with Palomino's talent, he counselled his going to Madrid. Befriended at the capital by Carreño and Coello, Palomino advanced rapidly in his profession. In 1683 he was chosen by Coello to assist him in his frescoes of Cupid and Psyche, in the Queen's gallery of the Alcazar. At Coello's death, Palomino was employed to assist Giordano in arranging the order and treatment of his work at the Escorial. He executed a number of weak frescoes at Valencia in 1697, and painted the dome of San Esteban at Salamanca, in fresco representing the Church Militant. In 1706, Palomino returned to Madrid, where he prepared the first volume of his *Museo Pictorico*, which appeared in 1715. This work, entitled *El Museo Pictorico y escala optica*, is in three parts ; the two first treat of the history, practice, and contain a summary of the general principles of art ; the third part is called *El Parnaso Español;* it is a collection of the biographies of Spanish painters from Antonio del Rincon down to Palomino's contemporaries. It lacks accuracy, and is cumbrous and long-winded, jumbling together the most incongruous materials, and often giving an explanation by no means just or clear. It has no classification of systems according to their scientific unity, and is of little worth in its criticism ; but it is a most valuable treasure-house for all later writers. From it, indeed, Cean Bermudez gleaned much of his wealth. It has won for Palomino the name of the "Spanish Vasari."

As a painter Palomino has little power : his pictures are feeble and theatrical, while his design is often good, his colouring and expression are cold, poor, and lacking in character.

Palomino died at Madrid in 1726.

After Giordano followed a host of foreign artists,—Tiepoli, Ranc, Hoovasse, Fremin, Paret, Van Loo, and the greatest of them the Saxon Mengs.

Anton Raphael Mengs was born at Aussig, in Bohemia, in 1728. He was a pupil of his father, Ismael Mengs, a distinguished painter on enamel and in miniature, who trained his son severely but thoroughly for his work as an artist. When but a mere lad he was sent to Rome, where he studied from the antique, and copied the great masters. He seems to have mastered every technical difficulty in his path, drawing, colour, chiaro-scuro; and to have lacked one thing only—an artist's soul. His thought was commonplace; his training perfect. His career reminds one of the stilt-mounted shepherds of *Les Landes*, who stride with rapid skill over vast spaces of barren sand.

In Mengs we have not merely an individual, but one who represents his class and his time; and rightly to weigh such a character, we must recall the condition of the Spanish nation. A people that in the seventeenth century could produce a Zurbaran and a Velazquez, and that in the day of Charles III. was measured by a Raphael Mengs, must have gone through a marvellous change. In its day Spanish art had towered above all others in grandeur, in reality. But long before the French yoke was fastened on its neck, the Spaniard had become enslaved by his own vices. Nature was no longer a power over the painter's heart; it was overlaid by a heap of academical traditions. Art was dwarfed into a round of petty imitation; and there was little left of the great fabric which Velazquez crowned but a tawdry pleasure-house.

David appears but a moment in Spanish history, but it is as the cold brain, the iron will that leads all the rest. With his affectation of the antique and his crimes against the laws of all good art, Spanish painters thought that he rose in grandeur above Velazquez.

"Modern Spanish art, the child of corrupt parents, carries from its birth a germ of weakness. Mengs, the incarnation of the academical mediocre, led the way; then followed David, fit painter of the Revolution, who trampled on the fine arts of cowed Europe. His theatrical scenes à la Corneille, his swaggering attitudinarian heroes *à la grande opera*, combined with a certain severity of drawing and a réchauffée of the antique, bewildered the R. A.'s, already predisposed in his favour by his Mengs-like style. To him, therefore, they turned submissively in spite of his want of real colour, air, nature, and *life*—the soul of painting; and the disciples, as is common in heresies, out-Heroded their master." [1]

We have followed, step by step, the growth and decline of Spanish art. We stand now at its death-bed. In the midst of the darkest and saddest age of Spanish history, when art is dead, and the nation itself, after years of inward decay, sits desolate and enslaved; when ribaldry is wit, and lust is love; when the national life seems blotted out forever, and not a ray of hope lightens the gloom of the future, the school of Mengs and David appears—the unschooling of all art.

And after Mengs and the French painters, what shall we say of their weak and servile imitators, the native artists? Juan and Nicolas Garcia de Miranda, Miguel Jacinto, Francisco Antonio, Josef Romeo, Geronimo Antonio de Ezquerra, Andres de la Calleya, Pablo Pernicharo, Luis, Alexandro, and Antonio Gonzalez Velazquez, Josef and Fernando Castillo, Maella, Aparicio,

---

[1] Ford, p. 748.

Francisco and Ramon Bayeu y Subias, and a host beside
—each one more affected and feeble than his predecessor;
such daubsters have no place in the history of Spanish
art.

Francisco Goya y Lucientes was born at Fuente de
Todos, in Aragon, in 1746. He studied painting awhile
under Luxan Martinez at Zaragoza, whence he went to
Rome. After several years passed in study he returned to
Spain, establishing himself at Madrid. He was employed
to make designs for the royal tapestry, and was thus
brought to the notice of Mengs, then at the height of his
fame. Goya won rapid recognition from the king and
court. In 1780 he was chosen member of the Academy
of San Fernando, and in 1795 a director. In 1789, when
Charles IV. came to the throne, Goya was made painter-
in-ordinary. He was a great favourite in the fashionable
world, and mingled in all the court intrigues. He was a
politician, a man of the world; neither better nor worse
than most around him. After the return of the ignoble
Ferdinand VII., Goya was suspected of revolutionary
ideas, but was permitted to retain his post as painter-in-
ordinary. He soon, however, retired in voluntary exile
to Bordeaux, where he died in 1828, at the age of eighty-
two.

Goya was a most prolific artist in every branch of art.
He has left important religious paintings, both in fresco
and on canvas. For one of the chapter rooms at Toledo
he painted the " Betrayal of Christ," a work of great

merit, displaying a marvellous effect of light and shade.
In 1778 he painted a "Christ on the Cross," now in the
Prado, for the church of San Francisco el Grande. It is
a noble composition, with clear, luminous colour, fine
touch, and true, delicate modelling—a great contrast to
most of his religious works. " They are in general either
commonplace or even feeble, or they are coarse and re-
volting. Of the former kind are his scenes from the life
of St. Francis Borgia, in the Cathedral of Valencia,
although one of them represents an occurrence likely to
have arrested his imagination—the soul of a dying sinner
seized in its flight by three hideous demons, who are discovered by a supernatural light flashing from the crucifix
of the ministering Jesuit. An example of his more forcible, but perhaps more disagreeable manner may be found
in his Sta. Justa and Sta. Rufina, in the sacristy of the
Cathedral at Seville, a picture in which, so far from seeking to catch the poetical aspect of his subject, he has
contented himself with meretriciously pourtraying, in the
virgin-martyrs, the not very refined courtezans who served
him as models." [1]

But he is, with all this, a man of strong native elements;
capable, if not of lofty religious enthusiasm, of poetic
grandeur ; of much brilliancy and genuine excellence. He
cannot paint an ideal saint, but he can lash the vices of
priest and courtier with keenest sarcasm. He holds up to
scorn the follies of worship and the corruption of the

---

[1] Stirling-Maxwell, pp. 1262, 1263.

cloisters. He parodies the *auto-da-fés* and the solemn
processions of his time; he never tires of painting the
lecherous friar or smooth rascal of a monk. He executed
a series of eighty prints, which he called *Caprichos—*
Whims. In them he holds up to ridicule the shams and
foibles of all classes—the thievish lawyer, the worldly
prelate, the obscene monk, the ignorant quack. He
touches with caustic pen the court scandals, not sparing
the queen herself, the infamous Maria-Luisa; and on
Godoy, the Prince of the Peace, he pours all the venom of
his biting satire. His pages are filled with grotesque
shapes, frightful monsters, grim devils, strange, mysterious, cloud-wrapt figures. In all he displays a weird,
fantastic humour.

His portraits are admirable, especially those of Charles
IV. and the Queen, in the Prado. There exist some two
hundred portraits by Goya: courtiers, poets, politicians,
fair ladies—all figure on his canvas. His work with the
graver is very famous. He etched the five equestrian
portraits, *Los Borrachos, Las Meninas,* and several of the
dwarfs and single figures of Velazquez. "He also published thirty-three prints of scenes in the bull-ring, being
illustrations of the national sport of the Peninsula, from
the days of the Cid and Gazul, the 'stout Alcayde' of the
ancient ballads to the death of Pepe Illo, the most dexter-
ous of *matadors,* and a writer on the sport to which he fell
a victim in the arena of Madrid. To these he added, during his residence at Bordeaux, and while deaf and nearly

blind, some lithographic prints of inferior merit indeed, but not devoid of his ancient fire." [1]

His historical pictures are very powerful, though they have their extravagances. In the Prado are two scenes charged with the horrors of that awful time when the storm of war swept over the city; and all hope was destroyed on the fatal *Dos de Mayo*, when the Mamelukes of Murat massacred their prisoners in the Puerta del Sol.

There is a most attractive series of twenty-seven pictures which was executed for the Villa Alameda ; they are woven out of the common incidents of social life,—comic dramas, simple pastorals, a dance by the river side, labourers resting, a winter landscape, a group of gypsies, and similar scenes. It is the heart of Madrid, the life of that gay city that we find in his *Romeria di San Isidro*, the great festa of the Madrilenians. They crowd the banks of the Manzanares ; the whole city is there ; you see the booths with their gay merchandise, you met that bustling tradesman but yesterday in the *Calle Mayor*. Those handsome cavaliers and superb Swiss are surely portraits. The fair señorita in her mantilla and coquettish fan, the gitanas with their tambourines, are drawn to the life ; it is a picturesque crowd of quarrelling, bargaining, gambling, drinking, dancing, laughing Spaniards. He brings the real Castile before you on his canvas. You walk through the long crooked streets, with houses six stories high, their balconies carved with most grotesque tracery ; broad

---

[1] Stirling-Maxwell, p. 1270.

plazas crowded with dirty, noisy children, old men sitting in ragged state, amidst the stench of the street, smoking in grave meditation ; processions of mourners following a bier with a plaintive howl ; horse-dealers, and the stalwart, swarthy *picador* with his gay sash, leading a fiery Bucephalus. His canvas gives us the last and fading view of the old Spain of romance and art.

It is the world of our old dreams. But the exacting faith that once reared those monuments, that scattered those marvels of religion and art over hill and valley in their profusion, has lost its power to command. All those creations of ecstatic fancy, those marvels of art that made this the wonderland of the West are only the relics of a faded past. The Gaul and the Briton have long ago pillaged these shrines ; monkish cupidity has helped on the iconoclasm of time, and left the saints legless and noseless ; and now only the churches and museums guard those treasures that are left. Yet amidst the twilight of those old cathedrals we can see again the mighty Past rise before us. We are like the dreamer in the Arabian legend, transported into the heart of the buried world, and behold the wealth of centuries. We see anew the dark crowds of worshippers as they knelt before the noble shrine ; the long procession of acolytes, as swinging the smoking censers, they wound along, chanting their hymns of praise, while the myriad tapers lighted up the dark aisles, and the wondrous groups that now look down on here and there a curious visitor.

INDEX OF SPANISH MASTERS.

A.

B.

www.ingramcontent.com/pod-product-compliance
Lightning Source LLC
Chambersburg PA
CBHW030734280326
41926CB00086B/1540